KING TOWNSHIP
200 0
BY: KATIE S.
THE QUEST OF THE NEW MILLENNIUM
I ♥ BOOKS
SHARE THE FUTURE!
PUBLIC LIBRARY

LAKE SIMCOE

and Lake Couchiching

LAKE SIMCOE
and Lake Couchiching

MARY BYERS

WITH PHOTOGRAPHS BY JOHN DE VISSER

The BOSTON
MILLS PRESS

Cataloging in Publication Data

Byers, Mary, 1933–
Lake Simcoe and Lake Couchiching

Includes bibliographical references.

ISBN 1-55046-269-5

1. Simcoe, Lake, Region (Ont.) – History. 2. Simcoe, Lake, Region (Ont.) –
History – Pictorial works. 3. Couchiching, Lake, Region (Ont.) – History.
4. Couchiching, Lake, Region (Ont.) – History – Pictorial works.
I. De Visser, John, 1930– . II. Title.

FC3095.L22B93 1999   971.3'17   99-930191-8
F1059.L22B93 1999

03 02 01 00 99   1 2 3 4 5 6

Published in 1999 by
BOSTON MILLS PRESS
132 Main Street
Erin, Ontario N0B 1T0
Tel 519-833-2407
Fax 519-833-2195
e-mail books@boston-mills.on.ca
www.boston-mills.on.ca

Distributed in Canada by
General Distribution Services Limited
325 Humber College Boulevard
Toronto, Canada M9W 7C3
Orders 1-800-387-0141 Ontario & Quebec
Orders 1-800-387-0172 NW Ontario & other provinces
e-mail customer.service@ccmailgw.genpub.com
EDI Canadian Telebook S1150391

Distributed in the United States by
General Distribution Services Inc.
85 River Rock Drive, Suite 202
Buffalo, New York 14207-2170
Toll-free 1-800-805-1083
Toll-free fax 1-800-481-6207
e-mail gdsinc@genpub.com
www.genpub.com
PUBNET 6307949

THE CANADA COUNCIL | LE CONSEIL DES ARTS
FOR THE ARTS | DU CANADA
SINCE 1957 | DEPUIS 1957

*We acknowledge for their financial support of our publishing
program the Canada Council, the Ontario Arts Council, and
the Government of Canada through the Book Publishing
Industry Development Program (BPIDP).*

Design by Gillian Stead
Printed in Hong Kong

Contents

Penetanguishene Road near Kempenfeldt, 1838, *by George Russell Dartnell.*
Inscribed on the mount, "Girdled Pines — a deserted clearing.
Near the village of Kempenfeldt. Lake Simcoe."

Introduction

If location is everything, Lake Simcoe has it. For centuries Lake Simcoe was the geographical liaison between Lake Ontario and Lake Huron, a route for native people, explorers and fur traders. Artefacts from the 1500s found near cottages at De Grassi Point offer proof that the lake was then a well-used stepping-off place to points north. Samuel de Champlain and Etienne Brûlé traversed its waters in 1615. In 1793, Lieutenant-Governor John Graves Simcoe first saw the lake he named for his father as he travelled up the western shore to the Penentanguishene Road, the Nattawasaga River and Georgian Bay. As well, there were alternate routes from the east side of the lake through the Narrows to Lake Couchiching and the Severn River. Sir John Franklin crossed and camped on Lake Simcoe en route to the west and a Northwest Passage.

A key entrance to Lake Simcoe was Holland Landing, the gateway to the lakes. Situated by the Holland River, it was the location of two landings, the upper landing, with access to an early fur-trade route to Newmarket, and the lower landing, where steamboats began their lake crossing. Holland Landing stood at the end of the old Toronto Carrying-Place Trail, the land and water link between Lake Ontario and Lake Simcoe, the main route following the Humber River. It was the site of the earliest mills in the area. Settlers were said to have walked to those mills from as far away as Flos, Tiny and Tay Townships near Georgian Bay. (John Graves Simcoe, having to name a multitude of townships, settlements and so on, and having used up the names of most of the military officers from home, finally, possibly in desperation, named these three townships after his wife's three dogs.) Early mail delivery around the lake began when someone set off on foot from Holland Landing. Convivial resting-places could be found in the town's many inns.

The names for this capricious body of water reflect its history. For Lake Simcoe there were many. To the Huron it was Ouentaron, "the beautiful lake." The French name was Lac aux Claies, or Le Clie, "lake of the fish weirs or fences," which refers to the fishing weirs at the Narrows. In Ojibway it was, among other names, Ashuniong. The Algonquin called it Wahweyagahmah, "round lake." A 1624 map identified it as Lake Toronto and the natives inhabiting its shores were Toronotogueronons. Maps in 1688 and 1744 altered that spelling to Lac Taronto. Finally it was named by Lieutenant-Governor Simcoe in honour of his father, Captain John Simcoe of the Royal Navy. Lake Couchiching (an earlier spelling was Gougichin) may mean "lake of many winds," but the word may also be from the Ojibway, meaning "little lake at the end of a big lake."

By 1822, Governor Peregrine Maitland had decided that, indeed, location was everything. Lakes Simcoe and Couchiching would be the hub of Ontario's water transportation system, an idyllic spot, tucked safely away from American attack, and the natural place for the capital of Upper Canada. He could see the site, the tiny village of Roches Point.

Residence of James Wickens, Lake Simcoe, 1836, by George Russell Dartnell. Inscribed on the mount, "Residence of Wickens, Esq. a Member of the Canadian Parliament in 1838 -! near Barrie on the North Shore of Lake Simcoe Kempenfeldt Bay." (James Wickens, a former lieutenant on the commissariat staff of the British army in the Peninsular War, was elected to the Upper Canadian Assembly in 1836.)

There were more schemes. With the commencement of work on the Trent Canal in the 1830s, there would be a route to the east, a link from Lake Simcoe to the St. Lawrence River. Since the early 1800s there had been many plans for a Hurontario Canal to run from the valley of the Humber up to Lake Simcoe and then on to Georgian Bay and Lake Huron. There was talk of a ship railway. It seemed that the lake was to be the gateway to east and west.

"But," said Stephen Leacock, "the real crown and glory of the route was its unexpected by-product, the settlement of the district. When the townships were opened settlers flocked up Yonge Street, they occupied the Oak Ridges and spread north among the pleasant hills and valleys where Newmarket now is, then reached the Holland River and so, in flat boats and scows, and presently in steamers, spread around the lake and through it around the bottom end of Couchiching."

Governor Colborne sought retired military officers as settlers. He saw their presence as providing a base for administrative, political and judicial leadership. Their rank did bring with it respect, and so they became the local gentry. In many cases they built estates that they named and patterned after the family manor house they had left behind. They brought their treasures with them, whether it was large pieces of furniture transported across the ocean and by wagon and ship to their forest home, or small pieces of silver emblazoned with a family crest.

There was excellent agricultural land to be had, but it was covered with dense forest. It was anything but easy for those first half-pay officers, used to comforts, and for immigrants and their families. Early diaries and letters indicate the struggle and the rewards.

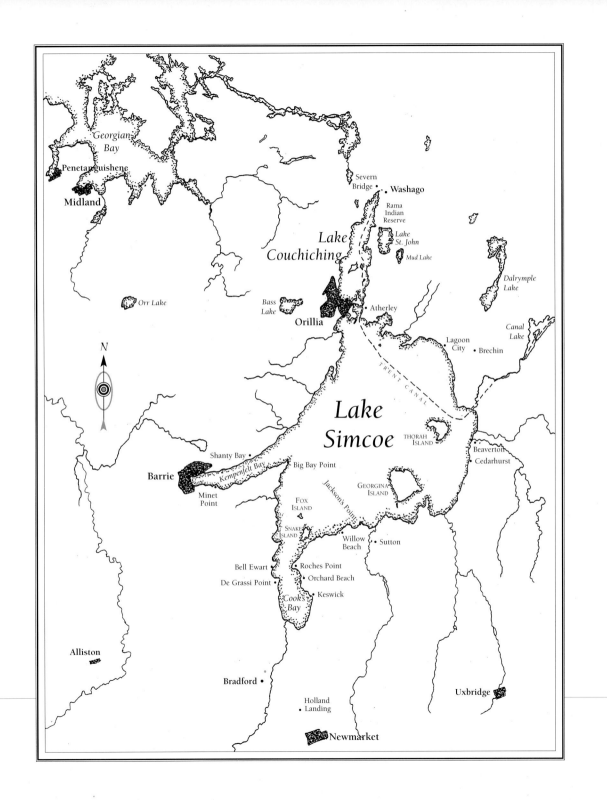

Georgian Bay

Penetanguishene

Midland

Severn Bridge

• **Washago**

Rama Indian Reserve

Lake St. John

Lake Couchiching

Mud Lake

Orr Lake

Bass Lake

Dalrymple Lake

• Atherley

Orillia

Canal Lake

• Lagoon City

• Brechin

N

Lake Simcoe

THORAH ISLAND

TRENT CANAL

Beaverton

• Cedarhurst

Shanty Bay •

Big Bay Point

GEORGINA ISLAND

Barrie

Kempenfelt Bay

Jackson's Point

Minet Point

FOX ISLAND

SNAKE ISLAND

Willow Beach

• Sutton

Bell Ewart

• Roches Point

De Grassi Point

• Orchard Beach

Cook's Bay

• Keswick

Alliston

Bradford •

Uxbridge

Holland Landing •

▪ **Newmarket**

Narrows of Lake Simcoe, June 13, 1830; William Marsh to his wife Susannah, who was staying near Sheppards Tavern, Yonge Street, York:

I have not been on a bed since I landed here or had all my clothes off but so natural is it become to me that I can wrap myself in a blanket and lie down on a piece of bark and sleep as comfortable as I could use to do on a feather bed.... On Wednesday last tho a very wet day I had to remove a few miles to a new station with bed etc on my back and on my arrival had to build a House for the night whilst it rained rivers, it was about as hard a rub as I have had and what made it worse my head aked and I was quite unwell for that and the next day.... There are from 150 to 200 Indians, men, women, and children, working on the road which is now nearly opened through, but I think we shall not be able to complete it according to Sir John's plan until we have had a little more frost and snow to soften the materials etc. there [are] three houses built at the Narrows only in one of which I am writing, it is inhabited by Mr. Phillips.... There are excellent traits in the Indian character among which are honesty, contentment, and good humour — in going through the woods from the Narrows to Metachdash I lost my pocket inkstand on the Indian path, several days after as Mr Lewes came that way he found it tied with a bit of basswood bark to a stick in the most conspicuous place with a view no doubt for the owner to get it again.

View of Barrie, Kempenfeldt Bay, 1841,
by George Russell Dartnell.

Lee farm, Lake Simcoe, August 13, 1838; Captain Simon Lee:

Many reports as to the rising of the rebels. [Anger against the Family Compact, which resulted in the Mackenzie rebellion, brewed on the shores of Lake Simcoe.] The country is in a very disturbed state. My watchdog shot at by buckskins at midnight on the 24th. Wolves much about on the lake, two very large ones were gambling about like dogs just out of gunshot two days earlier.

The capital remained at York. The Trent was the only canal to be completed, and the ship railway never developed. But by the mid-to-late 1800s a new transportation link was embracing the lake. Rail lines began to surround it. The first completed section of the Northern Railway was on the west side of Lake Simcoe, extending to Allendale. A window had opened. There was a developing lumbering industry to serve. The huge ice blocks being cut from the lake had to be transported around the continent. There was finally a chance to find real wealth. Bold entrepreneurs and colourful characters began to make their presence known in Barrie, the county seat for Simcoe, and in Orillia, where the Tudhope family had started to build motorized carriages.

Then cottagers started to come. They still do. After all, location is everything. Lake Simcoe's 300 square miles of water are surrounded by 140 miles of weaving shoreline, its bays and points wending their way through diverse communities. Campers and cottagers came first from Barrie and Orillia and then, in the late 1800s, the steady flow from

Toronto to this retreat began. Steamers, no longer in service as the only means of transportation, took tourists around the lake. It was the era of the rowing skiff. After sunset, Kempenfeldt Bay would fill with paddlers, their canoes equipped with all the comforts needed for a moonlight excursion. Regattas were ubiquitous. Champion oarsmen such as Ned Hanlan came to visit. Orillia native Jake Gaudaur raced there. The waterfront was lined with boatworks.

In winter and in summer many have waxed eloquent about these special lakes. But none said it better than Stephen Leacock did while fully intoxicated with the beauty of those waters, sometimes mellifluous, sometimes churning.

I understand that the Islands of the Aegean Sea have been regarded for centuries as a scene of great beauty; I know, having seen them, that the Mediterranean coast of France and the valleys of the Pyrenees are a charm to the enchanted eye; and I believe that for those who like that kind of thing, there is wild grandeur in the Highlands of Scotland, and a majestic solitude where the midnight sun flashes upon the ice-peaks of Alaska. But to my thinking none of those will stand comparison with the smiling beauty of the waters, shores and bays of Lake Simcoe and its sister lake, Couchiching. Here the blue of the deeper water rivals that of the Aegean; the sunlight flashes back in lighter colour from the sandbar on the shoals; the passing clouds of summer throw moving shadows as over a ripening field, and the mimic gales that play over the surface send curling caps of foam as white as ever broke under the bow of an Aegean galley.

What follows is a taste only of the history and beauty that have touched Leacock and countless others, the author and photographer included.

The old Penetanguishene Road today.

Orillia, from the Narrows.

Orillia

There is a site at Orillia that is as old as the Egyptian pyramids. Five thousand years ago aboriginal fishermen built the Mnjikaning (in Ojibway, the language of the Chippewa, meaning "fish fence") at the Atherley Narrows, the division between Lakes Simcoe and Couchiching. Wooden stakes, driven into the lake bed and interwoven with mesh, served to guide the fish to areas where they might be speared, netted or held. These weirs are still in the channel's depths today.

In Couchiching Park, on Orillia's waterfront, stands a magnificent tribute in bronze to a man who saw those weirs nearly four hundred years ago. The monument to Samuel de Champlain, the work of Vernon March (he later created the War Memorial in Ottawa) is one of the finest pieces of bronze statuary in Canada. It is said that 18,000 people came to Couchiching Park on July 1, 1925, for the monument's unveiling. Commemorating the three-hundredth anniversary of Champlain's visit to Huronia, the monument recalls the history of Orillia's beginnings, times of strife.

There was celebrating when Samuel de Champlain first visited Huron lands in 1615. He was welcomed by a people 30,000 strong, rich with good lands and agriculture. In Cahiagué, the largest community, he was shown 200 longhouses, which housed 5,000 residents. Champlain sought a partnership of Huron and French in peace with a conquered Iroquois. He led a Huron attack on Iroquois territory south of Lake Ontario. It failed. Defeated, he returned to Huronia. There he encouraged Jesuit priests to build missions, an act that further enraged the Iroquois, who resented French intrusion in Huron and Iroquois affairs. The stage was set for reprisal. That came eventually in vicious attacks that decimated the Huron. Then European diseases ravaged their people. The proud 30,000 were reduced to 300. It remained for the Chippewa, friends of the Huron, to banish the Iroquois and become the "people of the fish fence." Then, for another century, these lands were the well-travelled route of fur traders and explorers. Both weirs and monument are visible reminders of Orillia's ancient history, factious times.

In the early 1800s the seeds of further strife were planted with the help of the colonial government and a surge of settlers from the British Isles. Delighted to settle loyal men and women in the area, Sir John Colborne made way for them by grouping the Chippewa on Crown lands, partly on the Coldwater Trail, and partly in a native village on the present site of Orillia. Conflict heightened. The whites settled around the village but had no access to the lake. In 1836 they petitioned government for the native village. It became theirs. The Chippewa were dispersed. Many located on the other side of Lake Couchiching in the Rama reserve.

From these divisive beginnings the town grew at a slow pace. Then, during the nineteenth century, lumbering and the railways built Orillia. Logging was not new. Log booms were a familiar sight on the lakes. But the demand was growing apace. By mid-century it was huge.

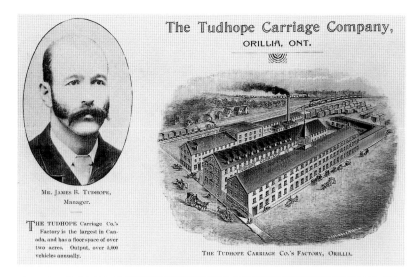

The Tudhope Carriage Company,
ORILLIA, ONT.

Mr. James B. Tudhope,
Manager.

THE TUDHOPE Carriage Co.'s Factory is the largest in Canada, and has a floor space of over two acres. Output, over 5,000 vehicles annually.

THE TUDHOPE CARRIAGE CO.'S FACTORY, ORILLIA.

One of the first Tudhope motor buggies.
What more would you want in a convertible?

The number of mills quadrupled from 1850 to 1870. Rails lines gave reliable transportation. Jobs were plentiful. Fortunes could be made. A select few grew incredibly wealthy.

Randy Richmond of the *Orillia Packet and Times* used the phrase "the Orillia Spirit" as the title of a book in which he describes the confidence and creativity that motivated some of Orillia's favoured few. In most cases a dash of bravado helped. Take, for instance, lumber baron Andrew Tait. He started making shingles with "a hand-powered machine" and one employee, his wife, who "bundled them up." When this fledgling enterprise grew into a huge milling operation, Tait needed a mansion to make a statement about his newfound wealth, and so he built Glenora. Richmond noted:

It is said that Andrew Tait built a tower on his mansion so he could watch his workers at his sawmill nearby. Employees worked from 6 a.m. to 6 p.m. for a dollar a day and Tait made sure they worked hard for that dollar.… He thought dancing was sinful, so instead of a ballroom, he built a roller skating rink on the third floor of his mansion to keep his children amused and out of trouble. He played on Lake Couchiching on his own steam yacht, sharing the waters with another of Ontario's most successful lumber kings, John Thomson.

And then there were William Tudhope, his sons, and their Tudhope Carriage Company. In 1909 they had what might have been a devastating, permanent setback.

Half a million dollars went up in smoke in less than two hours this afternoon, and as a result three hundred men are out of employment and a dozen families are homeless. At 2:15 p.m. an alarm of fire was sent in from Box 6, and it was immediately seen that the mammoth works of the Tudhope Carriage Company were ablaze, dense volumes of smoke arising from that

The Tudhope Carriage Company after the 1909 fire.

section of town. The run was only two blocks from the fire station, but by the time the brigade and hose waggon arrived flames were issuing from all the upper windows, and all four buildings were soon on fire. Several streams of water were quickly on, but it was soon realized that the factory was doomed, and the firemen turned their attention to saving adjacent buildings.... The Tudhope Carriage Company's plant, buildings, and stock were worth approximately five hundred thousand dollars, with insurance for somewhat less than half that amount.... Coming at this season of the year, the whole stock of cutters and sleighs for the ensuing season's trade was destroyed. The loss on motor buggies was also heavy. A very large exhibit had been prepared for the Toronto Exhibition, and would have been shipped on Monday.

The Globe, August 23, 1909.

It had been forty-five years since William Tudhope, one of nine children of a Scottish immigrant, had opened his blacksmith and wheelwright shop in Orillia. Five sons joined him in the business. They formed the Tudhope Carriage Company Limited, with James Brockett Tudhope as the head. Manufacturing wagons, carriages and cutters and, with a western associate, agricultural machinery, they had warehouses throughout the West and wholesale companies in eastern Canada. Moving with the times, the Tudhopes began assembling a motor vehicle in 1907, the Tudhope-McIntyre. These were the motor buggies destroyed in the 1909 fire. The value of the buildings and vehicles and the number of men employed tell the story of Tudhope's success to that point. But they do not tell the story of the Tudhope tenacity.

JAKE GAUDAUR. Jennet Gill was the sixth child of Jacob Gill, of Orillia. The Gill family was prodigious and athletic, including Harry Gill, North American track and field champion. Jennet married Frances Gaudaur, whose father, Antoine Gaudaur, a Métis, was believed to be Orillia's first settler. Their son, Jake Gaudaur, became a world champion oarsman, and held a series of aquatic duels with the fabled Ned Hanlan. In 1887 on Lake Calumet, near Chicago, Jake beat Ned for $5,000 and the North American championship. For the next decade he was virtually unbeatable, setting new records almost every time he rowed. In 1893, against an outstanding field, he set a new world's record at Austin, Texas, and bettered it the next year. In 1896, at age thirty-eight, Jake won the world's championship on the Thames. He received a triumphant welcome home in Toronto and was brought back to Orillia on the steamer *Islay* escorted by six other steamers.

FRANKLIN CARMICHAEL, a founding member of the Group of Seven. Born in Orillia in 1890, he worked for a commercial art firm in Toronto and during that time met at the Arts and Letters Club of Toronto with the other artists who later formed the Group of Seven. After studying in Antwerp, Carmichael returned to paint Northern Ontario landscapes. He taught at the Ontario College of Art, was a founding member of the Canadian Society of Painters in Water Colour, and the Canadian Group of Painters.

The dramatic setback did not deter progress. The evening of the fire, Tudhope took pen to paper and began to design a new plant, and this one on a grand scale. Seventy-nine days later a huge new building was complete. The builder proudly reported on December 6: "Brickwork started September 24th, finished December 3rd; bricks used 1,800,000; flooring 1,250 feet; roof finished December 6th, squares used 700…. The above constitutes a record for building operations in Canada." And later, "Machinery, steam power, heating, electric power and lighting all installed, woodworking departments in operation, buggies will be shipped January 18th." An addition was made in 1910 and the company became the Tudhope Motor Company with a new star on the line, the Everett 30, also known as the Tudhope-Everett and later as the Tudhope. The company existed until 1919. The *Orillia Packet* noted that "because of the construction zeal of one man, Orillia quickly achieved an industrial importance out of all proportion to its size."

Orillia's colourful citizens can lay claim to an impressive number of anything-but-ordinary firsts. The first medical plan in Ontario was set in place in Orillia. It was called the Red Cross Hospital. Healthy participants could buy into it for five dollars. This would guarantee them free hospitalization when needed. Buoyed by its early success, the hospital advertised that one lumberman "would have been fertilizing the daisies now if it had not been for the Red Cross Hospital." The hospital went broke, however, because those who could afford the five dollars would not go to the hospital, and those who would go could not afford the five dollars.

The town built the first municipally owned hydro-electric power plant. But this did not happen, according to Randy Richmond, without "province-wide ridicule," and "the near-drowning of the mayor and council" in a steamboat sinking. (The dignitaries took their wives on an inspection trip in the steamer *Syesta*. The steamer overturned in the 100-yard-long Sparrow Chute and sank, *Titanic*-style, straightening up briefly before being sucked under. No lives were lost.) Numerous accidents later, with the work well behind schedule, the town fathers decided to move in on the problem, organizing a raid designed to take over the plant. Retaliation followed and the *Orillia Packet* posed the question "Is this Civil War?"

One outstanding first was the adoption of daylight savings time, four years before it was declared a war measure across the country. The instigator was Mayor Bill Frost, the father of Premier Leslie Frost. Frost decided that daylight savings time had merits and, though the townsfolk were horrified and confused by the idea, decided to implement it. On the appointed day, a Sunday, Bill Frost became confused by his own dramatic new system and was one hour late for church. (From then on he was known as "Daylight Bill.") The confusion became contagious. "Some residents figured putting the clock ahead one hour meant they lost that hour permanently, every day, and would get less sleep." Others were more practical. "On

Monday morning, employees of the Hewitt Brothers trucking yard arrived at 7 a.m. daylight savings time, but sat around another hour, waiting for standard time to catch up before starting work."

For a town such as this, no ordinary town hall and jail would do. Orillia had its castle — the Orillia Opera House. Built on land donated by Goldwyn Smith, it was opened in 1895 after much dispute regarding the necessity of such a grand structure. It is a splendid building with a history of debate and debacle — "the politicians generally causing more ruckus than the criminals." For twenty years it served as market and town hall, and theatre, offering an enriched cultural life. But in 1915 it was gutted by fire. The refurbishing took two years. Later, its glory days over, it became a cinema and home, as the local tourist line goes, to a ghost who plays only when the theatre is empty — the Orillia phantom.

CITY HALL AND OPERA HOUSE.

Orillia's Grand Opera House. In 1997 the main auditorium
was dedicated to Orillia's own Gordon Lightfoot.

Perhaps the theatre technician, who dropped in one night and saw a figure at the piano attired in a coat, with gloves on his hands, thought it was indeed the ghost. And so he sat, and audience of one, and listened, unobserved, to a performance by Lake Simcoe devotee Glenn Gould. (In *Glenn Gould by Himself and His Friends*, John Lee Roberts writes, "In a Chinese restaurant in Orillia...they always turned off the pop music when Glenn walked in and put on the Gould recording of Bach's 'Goldberg Variations.'")

Stephen Leacock — a happy man.

Stephen Leacock

I n regard to the present work I must disclaim at once all intentions of trying to do anything so ridiculously easy as writing about a real place and real people. Mariposa is not a real town…"

The people of Orillia didn't believe him. They knew that Stephen Leacock, who lived in nearby Old Brewery Bay, was writing about them and they didn't like it. There was Mr. Golgotha Gingham, Mariposa's undertaker who never let the words "funeral" or "coffin," or "hearse" pass his lips, but chose rather "interments" or "caskets," or coaches;" the innovative Josh Smith, the 280-pound proprietor of Smith's Hotel, who got around the liquor commission's rules by turning his bar into a "real French Caff" with a high-toned "French Chief" who prepared and served la carte du jour; and Jefferson Thorpe, the barber who made a fortune in mining stocks though "the odd thing was that till he made money nobody took any stock in his ideas at all. It was only after he made the clean-up that they came to see what a splendid fellow he was. Level-headed, I think, was the term."

Robertson Davies said, "There is love in the portrait, certainly, and indulgence for the folly of humankind. But what community had ever acclaimed a man because he showed it to be merely human?"

Today he is celebrated as Orillia's own, his house a national historic site. Stevie Jr. sold it after his father's death, but the citizens of Orillia, by that time proud of their Mariposa connection, raised the money to buy back and restore the lovely building. Each year the Leacock Medal for Humour is awarded and his prodigious talent is celebrated in the Leacock Festival of Humour. In itself, this is Leacockian humour, somewhat reminiscent of the turnaround in Jefferson Thorpe's image.

Leacock was born in Swanmoor, Hants, England, in 1869. His mother, Agnes Emma Butler, was orphaned early and raised by members of her parents' scholarly families — three of her uncles were educators at the university level. She was a well-educated woman herself, cultured, and with the fortitude to carry on cheerfully while enduring a husband who could never support her. Peter Leacock, from a family who had made considerable wealth in a wine business in Madeira, won her consent to a secret marriage. This union was never really accepted by either family. He was seventeen, she twenty-two. The first of their eleven children was born seven months after the marriage. Peter, the youngest of three sons, had no prospects in England and "no special distinction in education or ambition," so his father insisted he make his way farming in the colonies. Peter was consistent. He failed each time, having absolutely no success at an occupation that required work. But his father was persistent, sending him to South Africa, Kansas, and to the last home the young family shared, a farm near Sutton, on Lake Simcoe. Peter drank, gambled and loafed, finally attacking Agnes, at which point son Stephen stepped in, put his father on a train and told him never to come back.

In spite of these troubled times it was here at Sutton that Stephen

The stalwart Agnes Butler Leacock. Howard Chapman, longtime summer resident of Sutton, whose grandfather and great-uncle founded the Belle Ewart Ice Company, notes that his family grew up as part of the same social community as the Leacocks. "The Leacock family were great characters and, when they were together, you could hear them roaring with laughter. They knew their mother's habits pretty well," he adds, "and when she sent them all outside to play, they were sure that she was getting the old trunk out from under the bed to count her money."

developed his deep love for his lake: "I have often and often written of Lake Simcoe; I know, with a few odd miles left out here and there, its every stick and stone, its islands and points, and I claim that there is in all the world no more beautiful body of water…"

Stephen's education began in a one-room school in Egypt, near Sutton. Agnes, not satisfied with the curriculum, first taught the children herself, then hired a tutor for her large family. Throughout her troubled marriage she was always able to get financial help from Peter's grandfather. This enabled her to send Stephen, the scholar of her brood, to Upper Canada College. He graduated as Head Boy and, after a degree from the University of Toronto, taught at the secondary school level. A Ph.D. at the University of Chicago led to the position of professor and head of the Department of Economics and Political Science at McGill. As Leacock wrote in one of his autobiographical pieces, *I'll Stay in Canada*, "I got quite a good job at McGill University and held it for thirty-five years. My life has been as simple as one of Xenophon's marches. But at least my jobs grew longer. The next, I think, will be what you'd call permanent."

In his article "The Erudite Jester of McGill," Trent Frayne described Leacock. "He had twinkling wide-set grey eyes, a great mop of shaggy hair that grew low on his wide forehead and his clothes had the appearance of having been slept in for a week. He wore a size seventeen shirt collar where a fifteen-and-a-half would have been ample, his suits were baggy and roomy and his tie was generally askew. There was a suspicion at McGill that the gown he wore to classes had come with the fixtures. His brother George once remarked that he was sure Stephen would have liked to get a haircut 'but he never thought of it.'"

While at McGill, Leacock published nearly a hundred scholarly articles and numerous books on an erudite range of subjects and was a popular lecturer, probably because the humour was never far from

A gathering at Old Brewery Bay.

the surface. The story goes that one father wrote Leacock, suggesting surprise that his son had been in Leacock's class for six months but seemed to have only a limited knowledge of economics. Leacock's reply was brief: "It must be heredity." Forced into mandatory retirement at sixty-five, Leacock mused that there was nothing wrong with his brain at sixty-five that there had not been at sixty-four.

Stephen Leacock wrote articles on a wide variety of subjects, on most of which he was an expert. As an economist he wrote *A Plan to Relieve the Depression in Six Days, Remove It in Six Weeks, and Eradicate It in Six Years*. This plan, it is believed, made its way to President Franklin Roosevelt, who availed himself of some of its wisdom. As a private citizen Leacock did not hesitate to make his views known.

The boathouse, Lake Couchiching.
This was Leacock's retreat, from which
his inimitable characters emerged.

When some of his chickens were stolen he wrote to Ontario's premier, George Henry:

Day Letter Telegram
The Prime Minister
Toronto
Dear Mr Henry Chicken stealing in this district growing serious Stop Am offering reward [$25] for apprehension of latest thief on my property Stop Would it be too much to ask you to investigate Stop Stephen Leacock

It was after his eminently successful academic career that Leacock began to write the body of humorous work for which he is loved. As British writer J. B. Priestly put it, "It is when he puts aside the cap and gown, lights a pipe and fills a glass, and begins to play the fool that he achieves originality, insight, distinction. It is here too, and not in the lecture-room, that he becomes thoroughly and most refreshingly Canadian." It was a kindly humour for the most part, ironic, satiric, brilliant and the stuff of spontaneous laughter. He became a sought-after lecturer, noting finally that he would have to learn Chinese to get a fresh audience.

The first of his humorous books, *Literary Lapses,* was published in England. It was followed by over thirty books including *Sunshine Sketches of a Little Town,* which made him the talk of the town of Orillia. Leacock wrote most of his humorous pieces in his beloved home on Old Brewery Bay. He loved the name. "You can judge your friends by that name," he once said. "If they don't like the sound of Old Brewery Bay they aren't your friends. On the other hand, I've known people to grow thirsty as far off as Nebraska just thinking about it." He wrote mainly in the boathouse, which housed a bed and desk and afforded a stunning view of Lake Couchiching. His first home there, a cabin built in 1908, grew by the year but was in turn outgrown. By the 1920s, Leacock and his wife, Beatrix Hamilton, were planning a larger house, a "charming English place." It was completed in 1928. Sadly it was never home for Beatrix. She had died of cancer three years earlier. Leacock moved in with his son, Stevie Jr.

The house has nineteen rooms, nine fireplaces, and a sizeable basement with a billiard room. The spirit of its jovial owner lingers in the house. It can be felt in the wine cellar in the basement that was always stocked to serve his own well-known habits and the prodigious numbers of people he entertained. Careful with his money, Leacock

boasted that he was able to hold a buffet for seventy-five people and feed them at a cost of seventeen and a half cents per head. His favourite chair, strategically placed in his living room, afforded him a view of the pantry via a perfectly positioned dining-room mirror. This way he could see whether his five servants were hard at work. And the impish side is apparent in the equally strategic placement of the telephone in a small enclave off the hall. Assuming privacy, the unsuspecting user would divulge all, not aware that holes in the wall, cleverly concealed by a sliding panel, enabled Leacock, in his study on the other side of the wall, to see and hear the whole proceedings, perhaps picking up some fodder for his next tale.

Leacock's love of the lakes found its way into much of his writing, both fiction and scholarly works:

Couchiching contrasts with Simcoe. It is a lake of beautiful islands, of broken vistas, of sudden and angry winds and of soft repentant calm. As it goes north its shores turn to rock, the smiling farm country is gone and with the valley of the Severn begins the rugged northland of rock and scrub, of bygone birch and shivering pine....Lake Simcoe retains all the peculiar romance that goes with the last of anything. It is the frontier of sunshine; beyond it is the north.

Strathallan, George William Allan's country retreat.

Kempenfeldt Bay

The arms that enclose Kempenfeldt Bay from Barrie to Big Bay Point on the south side, and through Shanty Bay towards Orillia on the north side, shield the deepest section of Lake Simcoe. And the Bay, not to be outdone by Loch Lomond, has its resident sea monster. David Soules, who settled permanently near the present-day Cedar Mount in 1823, claimed to have actually seen Kempenfeldt Kelly. Soules is reported to have made the following comments: "The first time ever I saw it was years ago. My brother and I were washing sheep down by the shore. We heard a loud splash in the water a short way out and, looking, saw a huge long thing go through the water like a streak. It went around a little point and we followed it. Apparently it had gone into the swamp around the point for when we got there we found a deep wide trail in the mud." Later, Soules added that he had seen the serpent again. It was lying on the shore and he described it as "having many huge fin-like appendages and being very large and very ugly-looking." Over the years Kempenfeldt Kelly may have retreated to the deepest part of the bay, in order to escape the present-day din on the waters above.

In the nineteenth century, small towns with mills, breweries and boatbuilding enterprises were thriving along these shores. The remains of logging shanties, wharves and mill foundations could be found for years. Then, when good road access to Barrie was opened in the early 1900s, cottages proliferated along the Bay, from Minet's Point, the closest picnic, camping, and swimming hole to the city, along the shore to Big Bay Point.

In 1928 the *Barrie Examiner* sent a reporter to visit some of these new summer homes and report on their prestigious owners. Among many he visited were the homes of C. A. C. Jennings, editor-in-chief of the *Mail and Empire*; Mrs. H. V. Blackstock of Toronto; Edmund Lally, county treasurer, who built a log house later expanded by his daughter and her husband, Dalton McCarthy, founder of the law firm McCarthy and McCarthy; Hewitt Bernard, a brother-in-law of Lady Macdonald, John A. Macdonald's second wife (she was the original owner of the grounds on which the homes of Mr. Justice Lennox of the Supreme Court of Ontario, and Sir John Aird, head of the Canadian Bank of Commerce, were located); A. H. F. Lefroy, a well-known author on Canadian constitutional law; and Mr. Sommerville, headmaster of the preparatory school at Upper Canada College in Toronto, whose property Wood End was rented by Group of Seven artist Lauren Harris.

But no summer residence impressed the reporter more than Strathallan, to whose builder he awarded "first cottager" honours. "In the early [18]60s Senator Allan built [a] log house…and came there to find retirement in the heat of summer. Thus at so early a date was the prestige of Kempenfeldt Bay as a summer resort recognized, and Senator Allan became the first cottager."

The honour of first cottager may well be true. That he was at least one of the first to escape to a retreat on the Bay is certain. The site on which the cottage was built, 600 acres of lakefront, had been part of a 1,000-acre Crown grant to William Allan in 1821, to which he added in 1856. Allan, prominent businessman, judge, militia officer and

The "old cottage" at Strathallan.

member of the Legislative Council, owned thousands of acres of land including his home, Moss Park, in Toronto and all the land between Richmond, Bloor, Sherbourne and Jarvis Streets. He made no use of the spectacular site on Kempenfeldt Bay, still a forest, but his only surviving son, the Honourable George William Allan, built a residence there. (Allan's wife died of consumption as did nine of their eleven children, none of whom reached the age of twenty.) G. W. Allan escaped to the Bay as often as possible — first to his log house and then to Strathallan, his manor house. Constructed in the English style, Strathallan was built of lumber from the property, layer on layer of pine forming "a solid wall of pine a foot in thickness." The exterior was then stuccoed, so that the house was cool in summer and cozy in winter. For cold storage in summer the ice house held 300 blocks of ice that had been hauled up from the bay in winter by horse-drawn sleigh.

Diaries tell the story of the Allan family's life there. Allan reached Strathallan by train from Toronto to Allandale then by boat in summer and sleigh in winter.

Saturday, February 13, 1892, Strathallan:

Very cold morning — but bright sunshine — off for Strathallan at 8 o'clock. Heard to my surprise from the Conductor, that all trains north of Barrie had been stopped by the drifts yesterday.... However Hardie [resident caretaker at Strathallan] made his appearance all right although he said he had nearly upset several times between our gate and Painswick Corner. The sleighing was splendid on the Penetanguishene Road which was well beaten — but when we got to Painswick our troubles began and it was hard work going on from there. However we managed it without an upset although the drifts were very bad.

On October 30, 1892, G. W. Allan wrote to his daughter Maye, the wife of Herbert Harcourt Vernon. "Dearest Mayebird, I don't know a more fitting occasion than your Birthday, for giving you, with ever so much love, a deed of Ten acres on Strathallan, which I hope will be a happy summer home for many a long year, for you, and Herbert, and your children.... Your loving father." Ladywood was built that year on the northeast corner of the Strathallan property. It was designed by Toronto architect Frank Darling and stood there for 106 years, until demolished in 1998.

Near Strathallan and Ladywood, Major-General Donald Hogarth built a massive summer lodge with an unusual plan. Each room extended from the front to the back of the house, offering views of the lake and the woods and capturing northern and southern light. Hogarth's business career was in the resource industry; Steep Rock Mine was his greatest achievement. The lodge reflected his success — a large living room with huge pine beams and stone fireplace, a four-car garage and a private golf course (now the Allandale Golf Course). The

Mary (Maye) Adelaide Harcourt Vernon.

Ladywood, 1906.

lodge was bought by the Ontario government in 1968 and in 1982 became the Kempenfeldt Conference Centre for Georgian College.

The *Barrie Examiner*'s intrepid reporter directed his travels to the opposite shore of Kempenfeldt Bay, finding, at Fisherman's Point, that one James Yair, "endeavoured to boom that bit of shore as a summering place" by building himself a summer cottage that he called Casa Loma. Such a grand design set the tone for others. Certainly Woodlands could have carried such a prestigious name. "Large and beautiful trees adorn most of the sixty-nine acres comprising

Woodlands and through trees from the lakeshore road to the waterfront stands the house arustle [with] forest-like drive[n] winds."

The first name on the title of the Woodlands site is that of "William Davenport, A Man of Colour." Davenport got a Crown grant of 100 acres in 1828 as part of the Wilberforce Street settlement, land offered to Black veterans of the War of 1812. Wilberforce Street was one concession east of the Penetanguishene Road. Both settlements were designed to provide loyal resident strength in the event of American attack via Georgian Bay. The first free Crown grants to Blacks

Major-General Donald Hogarth's summer home (main house, above, and terrace below), now the Kempenfeldt Conference Centre for Georgian College.

Donald Hogarth with a church group in the 1940s.

Mr. and Mrs. William "Billie" Price, Madge Hogarth, the Honourable George Drew, premier of Ontario.

began in 1819, each document including the words "Man of Colour." But efforts to farm what was poor, swampy land resulted in the eventual sale of many of the lots. Their owners took jobs as farmers or loggers. An old will shows the efforts of one George Darkman to pass on an interest in his property by leaving the land to his wife or sons "provided they make their appearance on my estate within five years after my decease." They never did. By the 1900s the Wilberforce Street community had declined and virtually vanished. What remains is their church. The African Episcopal Church was built of log in 1848. It has been maintained over the years, wooden pulpit and pews still marked by their stark simplicity.

Parts of Davenport's property were subsequently sold and the 69 acres on which Woodlands stands passed through several hands until, in the late 1880s, a Mr. Powers built a dominating Victorian Gothic house there, a notable presence on Kempenfeldt Bay.

African Episcopal Church, Oro.

Powers' house was "one of the fine places on the lake [which] is also one of the largest. The house, a handsome brick structure, contains twenty-three rooms and is suitable for use in winter as well as summer. Central Ontario Hotels Ltd. plan to convert it into an all-year round tourist hotel to be known as Kempenfeldt Inn. The home was built by the late Mr. Powers nearly forty years ago. For some time it was the property of the late D. Crawford of St. Louis, Mo. who disposed of it to Col. A. G. Peuchan, the present owner, fifteen years past."

Colonel Peuchan could make one claim that could only be made by a few hundred people. He was a passenger on the *Titanic* on her fatal maiden voyage and he survived to tell the tale. The story goes that he was asked to help in the second lifeboat to be lowered into the icy sea. The boat was half empty and being lowered, so Peuchan swung by a rope to land in the small craft. According to Alan Hustak in *Titanic: The Canadian Story*, "As soon as he was aboard, the crewman in charge, the *Titanic*'s lookout Frederick Fleet, ordered Peuchan to help him get the rudder operating." Peuchan then grabbed an oar and "we rowed away like good fellows." Among the lifeboat's other lucky passengers was a woman who became a legendary character — the unsinkable Molly Brown. She took an oar and showed some other women how to use one. Peuchan later stated that he had urged their helmsman to go back to try to pick up some of the screaming men, women and children out of the ocean but that he had refused. Molly Brown was adopted by the press when she returned to New York and continued to make the most of her escape. Peuchan, on the other hand, paid dearly for the rest of his life for having survived when women and children died. One Shanty Bay woman remembered that town residents would cross to the opposite side of the road to avoid him.

Woodlands never did become the Kempenfeldt Inn. It was sold to Harold F. Ritchie, owner of a successful import-export business and

Eno Fruit Salts. Ritchie enjoyed the fifty-year-old home, with its fourteen-foot ceilings, ornate plaster-work, dramatic chandeliers and imposing mantelpieces, but added some practical amenities such as indoor plumbing and a central pump in the basement that ran giant refrigerators. One of Ritchie's daughters, Pauline, married Toronto lawyer Beverley Matthews. Woodlands is still in the family today.

When the Barrie reporter came to describe another grand estate, Senator Nicholls' magnificent Parklands, he could no longer control his verbosity. He effused:

[Nicholls] lavished money on the place and had erected a residence which is the most pretentious of any on the Bay or Lake. Senator and Mrs. Nicholls and their family had a wide circle of friends whom they entertained extensively. Although this luxurious home contained seventeen guest rooms it was found necessary to fix up another dwelling on the place for use as an annex…. There is a private wharf on which is located a steel lighthouse…. After occupying this beautiful home for eight years Senator Nicholls sold it to a syndicate from whom it was purchased by J. B. Holden, secretary of the Hollinger gold mines. For the past four years Mr. and Mrs. Holden have been the residents.

All that remains of Nicholls' and Holdens' Parklands today is the steel lighthouse, but the tradition of summer homes in the grand style is alive on Kempenfeldt Bay today.

The plaque in old St. Thomas' Church in Shanty Bay reads: "In loving memory of Edward George O'Brien who died September 8, 1875, age 76; and of Mary Sophia, his wife, who died October 14, 1876, age 78. This stone is raised by their children. He having served his country by sea and land, became A.D. 1830 the founder of the settlement and mission of Shanty Bay. She was a true wife and zealous in all good works. Faithful servants, they rest in hope."

Behind these simple words is a story of a pioneer and his wife — he a half-pay British officer of both the army and navy who decided to locate in Upper Canada, she "of landed gentry" from Britain's West Country. Mary Sophia Gapper had emigrated with her mother to Thornhill, where two of her brothers had recently located. She met Edward there and they were married in 1830. Two years later, with their first child, they moved to what was a relative wilderness, the north side of Kempenfeldt Bay, so that O'Brien could supervise the settlement of the government-sponsored Black community in Oro Township. When the O'Briens arrived in what would become Shanty Bay, the original land grants of 1819 had attracted a Black community of nearly a hundred.

Mary and Edward founded the community of Shanty Bay and historic St. Thomas' Church. The young bride kept journals and the record of their adventures takes on life in her words. The couple stayed on the south shore of Kempenfeldt Bay and lodged at the home of James Soules while being transported daily over the ice to where their shanty was being built.

April 5, 1832. Next morning we were rapidly transported across the ice on two sleighs with the whole contents of our wagons and half a dozen men whom we took over to commence operations. The sun shone so blandly and the air felt so warm on the dry bank where we landed that we hardly felt the want of the fire which the men had begun to kindle. Baby [William Edward, or "Willy"] was presently rolling in delighted freedom on the dry leaves, and the men with Edward dispersed on the level above which was still covered with snow, seeking a favourable situation for our shanties…the sound of the axes soon began to sing through the woods…. By the evening the walls of our dwelling — a double shanty — were completed.

They returned across the bay for the night's lodgings and made the crossing again the next day but:

A shout from across the lake attracted our attention and we heard that the oxen, which we had sent for from the other side, had got into the crack which they had to cross. This lay at about two miles distance. Instantly all hands about me started off to the scene and I ran up to the shanty to tell Edward…. They returned to safety with the oxen…. Our Negro neighbour who lives in sight of the place where the accident occurred went out too…. It was now too late to allow us any option as to where we should pass the night or even for the men to return to their homes. To them, therefore we assigned the less finished half of the shanty with all the spare bedding, which had been destined to complete our walls. They lighted a large fire on the ground and were soon wrapped in smoke and slumber…. We have begun to build another shanty for a man whom we have hired who has a wife and children. A little farther on Edward has given Hunt leave to make a settlement, so that we shall have quite a little village around the bay. We call it Shanty Bay.

May 5. One of the men we have at work is a great friend of Edward's. He is a runaway slave from the States where he had left a large family of children whom he expects to be able to get to him as soon as he has prepared a home for them and earned money enough to go back as near their neighbourhood as he can venture to continue their escape. He is a man of great respectability and command amongst the men of his colour.

In the summer of 1832, Edward and Mary began to build their permanent home and "The next day Edward sent for me to come, armed with a bottle of whiskey, to see the foundation logs of the house laid in their places — an operation of some nicety." They drank to the success of the house, giving it the name of Cedargrove Hall. The name was later changed to the Woods.

During their first summer at Shanty Bay the second of their six children, Lucius Richard, was born. (Mary O'Brien had three sons and three daughters between 1831 and 1840.)

August 15. [Awoke at dawn] to strange and ominous sensations. Edward set to work to get the stove up and I lay as quiet as I could on the sofa to wait till they had finished their work. After dinner I went to Mama's room to get out of their way and from thence I did not very immediately return, for a few minutes made me the mother of another son."

A Shanty Bay mission had been founded in 1830 and the construction of a parish church was very much on the young couple's minds. But even with generous gifts from England it took time to collect funds. Eventually £400 was raised. Edward gave forty acres of land for a church, rectory and school, and construction started. Mud brick, a mixture of clay and straw trampled by oxen in a pit into the right consistency, was the building material. This was later plastered over. The cornerstone was laid on June 19, 1838, and the O'Briens "assembled a party of about twenty or thirty to whom we gave a dinner, and, notwithstanding a little jam of discordant feeling, the whole was satisfactory and pleasant." (Mary and Edward objected to the trustees' plan to have private pews for those who had given the endowments.) The original square pews are still in use at St. Thomas,' as is the 1892 organ, the operation of which depended on help from a volunteer who pumped the handle, which was connected with the bellows. The organ was rebuilt in 1938 so this volunteer operation is no longer necessary.

In the 1840s, Lieutenant-Colonel Edward O'Brien (the militia appointment came after he formed his own company, the 35th Simcoe Foresters) and Mary moved to Toronto. Their eldest son, William Edward, became lieutenant-colonel, commanded the York

Lucius O'Brien.

"I don't say that my boy [Lucius] is an artist, but he sometimes torments me very inconveniently to supply him with implements to 'dera, dera.' Sometimes by the same passion I get him off my hands for an hour altogether. The productions of his pencil as far as I can judge are very much like and quite equal to those of any young gentleman of a year and a half old. Just now nothing will serve him but a pen and ink which is not quite convenient."
Mary O'Brien, February 12, 1834.
Lucius Richard, the O'Briens' second son, became a well-known artist and the first president of the Royal Canadian Academy, 1880–1890.

Etienne Jean, July 1, 1892, *by Lucius O'Brien.*

York Simcoe Regiment on the march to Humboldt to join Middleton at Batoche, Touchwood Trail, Fort Qu'Appelle.
Colonel William Edward O'Brien of Shanty Bay on the white horse.

and Simcoe Batallion in the Northwest Rebellion, and represented Muskoka in the House of Commons. Their second son, Lucius, with architectural and engineering training, was acknowledged to be Canada's foremost artist of the day. He was the first president of the Royal Canadian Academy. Four of Lucius O'Brien's paintings are in the National Gallery. Henry, a lawyer, edited the Canadian Law Journal. He founded the Argonaut Rowing Club.

William inherited and lived in the Woods. After his death it became the property of his daughter and her husband, E. V. Wilson. It was destroyed by fire in 1925.

Forest meets lake in autumn.

Samuel de Champlain, in bronze,
looks out over the water route he travelled in 1615.

Orillia's lights sparkle at dusk.

The glory days of rail remembered at the Ossawippi Express Dining Cars, Orillia.

Geneva Park, the YMCA summer school started in 1903 by Howard Crocker, physical director of the Toronto Central YMCA, and C. M. Copeland, coach of Canada's 1908 Olympic team and the acknowledged leader in physical training in Canada. The Lake Couchiching site was first used in 1907, then, thanks to funds from a group of businessmen, became the property of the YMCA, as it remains today.

The Orillia Fair celebrates a heritage passed down from early settlers.

Stephen Leacock's home on Old Brewery Bay.

The prestige of a "private" lighthouse, Kempenfeldt Bay.

The staircase at Woodlands, Shanty Bay.
Once the home of Colonel Peuchan, a Titanic *survivor.*

St. Thomas', built of mud brick in 1838.
The pioneer O'Brien family persevered until it became a reality.

The Narrows, Lake Couchiching, at Atherley, the link between the lakes.

Fern Resort, Lake Couchiching. The name came from an old log cabin, which was built on fern-covered rocks and known as Fern Cottage.
After the hermit who inhabited the cabin died, the McBain family built on the island and welcomed visitors at their table.
When the McBains moved to Orillia they leased the business, eventually to the Pettapiece family. The fifth generation of that family is at Fern today.

A quiet paddle, away from boat traffic.

An autumn sunset at Jackson's Point.

The War Memorial, Barrie.

*A revitalized shoreline
dominates the bay at Barrie.*

A summer's day at Barrie's waterfront.

Barrie

arrie's imposing site, at the head of Kempenfeldt Bay, speaks to its significance. It was a strategic location in the route between Lake Ontario and Lake Huron. Centuries ago, native people, fur traders, Jesuits and explorers stopped there. The route from York, up the Holland River to Holland Landing and along the west side of Lake Simcoe, led to the Nine Mile Portage, the route to Willow Creek, the Nottawasaga River and Georgian Bay. Barrie became a magnet on Kempenfeldt Bay due to its geographic location.

A writer for *The Globe* visited Barrie in 1842, when the town was preparing to take on its role as county seat with a newly built courthouse and jail, having been chosen for that honour over the nearby village of Kempenfeldt. This was only a dozen years after the first pioneer settlers came to build cabins there. It seems that by the time of the young traveller's 1842 visit, the place had already developed its reputation for rearing rugged individuals.

On enquiry I was told if I wanted to leave civilisation to make for Barrie, the jumping-off place.... On first entering town a strange-looking building attracted my attention; it was a large frame building constructed of heavy timbers and filled with complicated machinery from bottom to top. On enquiry I found that one John McCausland had spent years of his life in useless labour constructing it with the certain conviction that he was destined by fate to solve the problem of perpetual motion...everything comes to an end and so did Mr. McCausland's money and consequently his work at the motion, which

remained standing there for years, a monument to his folly.... [Other notables of the town included] John Watt, County Clerk, store-keeper, postmaster, and ready for anything else you wanted doing, even, in the parson's absence, to christening a baby or reading the burial service over a poor defunct, decidedly the most popular man of the town [and] Thrift Meldrum [who] was the crier of the courts, and many a time by his drolleries made Bench and Bar forget their dignity.

Another reporter for *The Globe,* visiting fifty years later, in 1895, was so overwhelmed by Barrie's charms that he reached for his ultimate accolade and compared it to Rome. The eternal city "sits on her seven hills," while beautiful Barrie "sits on a series of amphitheatre terraces, formed by the receding waters of an ancient inland sea." In case this was not praise enough, he went on to compare Barrie favourably with Naples, claiming that the town "leaves a lasting impression," and "has been called more than once the 'Naples of America' by eminent travellers." And there was more. Barrie was heaven for fishermen and hunters and one of the healthiest towns in Canada due to "the position it occupies affording the very best natural drainage, the cleanliness of its streets, the taste displayed by its citizens in keeping their places neat...the pure water from their artesian wells and...the cool exhilarating air that is always floating around it even on the hottest days."

All of this would no doubt have amused those who knew that Barrie had also been called the town with more taverns per head than

Barrie, 1875.

any in Canada. This latter honour may have come about because by 1832, five years before the hamlet's population had reached the grand total of thirty-six, including every man, woman and child, there were two taverns, Richard Carney's and John Bingham's, each one doing a brisk business. The ratio of tavern to drinking inhabitant in Barrie was formidable, albeit assisted by toping travellers.

By the close of the nineteenth century, Barrie had taken on a new look. There had been a twenty-year window — 1850 to 1870 — during which the town became a conduit from Lake Simcoe to Quebec City and one of the most vital lumbering centres in Ontario. The Ontario, Simcoe and Huron Union Railroad Company line (now the CNR) had been completed to nearby Allandale in 1853, with a station to Barrie

twelve years and much hyperbole later. Allandale had been amalgamated with Barrie in 1897. Railroad magnate F. W. Cumberland had once predicted that Allandale would have streets paved with gold while Barrie's would be full of grass, but now the gold appeared to be Barrie's for the taking.

Part of the change in Barrie's look was due to the arrival of judges, prominent businessmen and politicians who had moved to the county seat. John A. Macdonald, Canada's first prime minister, visited frequently and no doubt received free advice on running the relatively new Dominion. And in 1919 the railway that had brought such prosperity brought a royal visitor to Barrie. The Prince of Wales, the future Edward VII, left North Bay by rail at 5 a.m. and arrived in

Hamilton at 2:30 p.m. on the same day, having been viewed by the residents of thirty-four locations and making only three stops, one of which was in Allandale.

Commanding towers and turrets, bargeboard, airy and decorative but sturdy as well, curious chimneys and highly creative architectural features, including the use of crushed glass, offer evidence of the wealth and character that resided in this town and the status of those who strode across the local scene in the Rome (or Naples) of Lake Simcoe. On the highest of Barrie's several terraces, looking over the town from an imperious view, stands "Lount's Castle," built in 1878 for William Lount. From the windows of the turreted castle, Lount, a member of parliament and a judge of the High Court, had a commanding view of the affairs of the town. Ornate on the exterior and interior, the house included a ballroom. The elevated status of Lount's Castle made a statement about the elevated status of the man

G. T. R. Depot, Allandale.

Grand Trunk Railway depot, Allandale.

Lount's Castle.

Ardraven.

North. Not only did he become a right-hand man to John A. Macdonald but there was a family connection as well. McCarthy had been married five years previously to the widow of Macdonald's brother-in-law. Various words could be used to describe McCarthy's political career, not all complimentary, as he pushed the boundaries of the right wing a little further in that direction and engaged his many talents in a fight for a strong confederation, which he saw threatened by conflict with French Canada. His became notorious for his flaming rhetoric with such proclamations as "One Quebec is more than enough." McCarthy's house was like the man — expansive, imposing, and occupying a large space on the local scene. It can be seen at 5 Wellington Street East.

Another who was known for building a reputation and a house on a grand scale was Judge James Robert Gowan. His mansion, Ardraven, stood by the lake on Kempenfeldt Drive. It had an expansive verandah and a sensational view. At the time of the *Globe* article, Judge Gowan had just received his appointment to the Bench from the Baldwin government. Gowan was only twenty-eight and may have been the youngest lawyer in the country's history to receive a judicial appointment. The reporter called him "a bare-faced looking stripling, in appearance like anybody but a grave judge." He lived to ninety-four and assisted Macdonald in establishing courts and writing the statutes governing criminal law in Canada. He was made a senator, and knighted.

Oily Tom McConkey, named as much with admiration as derision for a consummate politician, lived at 101 Clapperton Street. With Jim Sanford (55 Peel Street), he built Barrie's Grand Opera House, which gained the admiration of the *Globe*'s reporter (who may not have known of or neglected to mention the $80,000 shortfall in Sanford's accounts for the building).

— a position he had reached in spite of the fact that there was a notorious rebel on his family tree. William's uncle was Samuel Lount, second in command to rebel leader William Lyon Mackenzie when, in 1837, the rebellion that had been brewing around the shores of Lake Simcoe shook the Family Compact in downtown Toronto. The shots that were fired on Yonge Street had been practised in vacant fields around the lake. William Lount's Castle is at 25 Valley Drive.

The year that Lount's Castle was completed, D'Alton McCarthy, a Barrie lawyer, was elected to serve as the Conservative MP in Simcoe

"It has a seating capacity for 1,200 persons, with boxes, cloakrooms etc. provided for the public. The sloping floors and galleries are admirably arranged, so that from every seat in the house there is a full view of the stage. The stage may be said to be a model, capable of accommodating scenery of any travelling company..... The whole house is thoroughly heated and ventilated and is lighted by 300 incandescent electric lights and decorated in fibrous plaster, picked out in warm, quiet colours. This will enable the best show companies on the road to visit Barrie."

Among the many other fine buildings that can be identified in several walking tours, with heritage maps set up by and available through Heritage Barrie, is the home of lumberman David Rees, who came to Barrie from New Orleans each summer to his estate, Glen Ormond, by Kempenfeldt Bay. Rees made the trip in his own railway car with his wife, Lautie, and a host of servants. The house, the second on the property, dates from 1895. Among more than seventy others on the walking tours are the homes of Patrick Lynch, who started as a brakeman for the railway in Allandale and became superintendent of the North Bay Division of the Grand Trunk Railway; Simon Dyment, whose success in the lumber business allowed him to participate in the sport of kings with the result that the Dyment's Brookdale Stables bred several winners of the King's Plate in the early 1900s; and Frederic Gore, who, with his wife, lived in and ran his grammar school at 47 Rodney, taking on a couple of dozen boarders in residence. Gore sold the house to Benjamin Walker Smith, who became a hero (or not, as your politics dictated) in Barrie. Smith saved the life of Canada's prime minister, John A. Macdonald, and numerous Conservative politicians when the steamer on which they were touring nearly struck rocks in Georgian Bay. Another grand home was Inchiquin, the most expensive house in town. It took six years to build and

Inchiquin.

became the home of William E. O'Brien, the son of Colonel Edward and Mary O'Brien of Shanty Bay. Construction was supervised by the groom's parents.

The Barrie of the late twentieth century has spread in all directions to satisfy a population that has grown from 800 in 1850 to over 90,000 today. It became a city in 1959, basked in the fame of its revitalised waterfront and the title of Ontario's Most Progressive City, and became a household word for the world-class Mariposa Skating School, where Brian Orser, Elvis Stojko and other Canadian and British champions have trained. And yet with the present so visible and vital, the past remains in Barrie's built history and in tales of the dominating characters, some noble, some not, who made the city their home.

The Islay *brings a crowd to the Big Bay Point dock.*

Big Bay Point

No place, however charming, can offer the summer vacationist more inducements or make better promise of a joyous holiday than Big Bay Point.... There are summer homes of every type present, some large; others small; a few weather beaten; many with the appearance of newness unsullied. All are decorated with gaudy pennants, or flashing banners. Varsity colours are numerous, McGill is represented and so occasionally are Harvard and Yale. Flaming cushions and wicker chairs give the place a holiday touch.... Throughout the length of the warmer days the beach is a scene of splashing, laughing and colourful gaiety.... At night the amusement consists of boating or dancing." These were the halcyon days of the early 1900s in this sought-after vacation spot!

But cottagers from Barrie and Toronto were far from the first to discover the point at the tip of Kempenfeldt Bay. Trails cutting off the point's tip acted as a shortcut for native people, explorers, even the acclaimed Sir John Franklin on his way to find a Northwest Passage, and then government officers taking supplies to Penetanguishene.

A century before the "wooded shores resound[ed] to the merry din of happy cottagers," an Irishman, Francis Hewson, the first settler at the Point, was swinging his axe on those same shores, building a log house and trying to control the obstacle to his plans for fields of wheat, the oaks and hemlocks that stood on his 500 acres. The wooded glades that so entranced cottagers later were not just a nuisance but a life-threatening hazard for a lone settler. Family tradition was that Hewson's dog, Sultana, saved his life on many occasions. When Hewson said "Sultana, I am lost," the dog led him home. Hewson became a magistrate and in that capacity performed most of the marriages between Holland Landing and Penetang. The first name given to the point was Hewson's Point.

The Hewsons were alone until the widow Achsah Soules arrived with her family. A United Empire Loyalist from Nova Scotia, she relocated after the death of her husband. Her son David bought 400 acres adjoining the Hewsons. Once again the impact of the forest was felt. Another of her eight sons, James, died there in 1833 when he lost his way and froze to death. Soon George Warnica, "The Dane," and his family arrived. He had left home at age eighteen to travel the world, met a widow in Syracuse and found his way with her to the Point area. Two of his four sons, George and William, made their mark by hacking out Yonge Street through the bush from Churchill to Barrie at five dollars per mile. The next year they completed the section down to Bradford. William married Sarah Orchard and produced thirteen children; from them came a family that still remains at Big Bay Point.

In 1837, gangs of men came calling at the Point. The story was related by young Samuel Lount Soules about his famous uncle, rebel leader Samuel Lount, a popular man who "was chosen to take charge of all the insurgents that could be collected from the northern townships." When the rebellion was crushed, Lount fled with four thousand dollars reward money on his head. Men took up the search

Isaac Robinson, farmer cum innkeeper, took to the hospitality business when farming proved unrewarding. Starting with a small operation, probably in his home, he prospered in his new role as innkeeper and built his impressive Robinson House, welcoming guests by 1887. Buoyed by the response to his two-storey frame hotel, he built his own dock nearby, at which he landed guests in his own steamer. Robinson lost out to the competition, however, when the grander Peninsular Park Hotel was built on land he had once owned.

The competition — the Peninsular Park or Big Bay Point Hotel, more spacious and elegant than Robinson House, for the ultimate in a summer vacation.

and, Samuel Lount Soules recalled, a gang came to his home, looted it, and thrust their bayonets into any possible hiding place. Young Soules was on the receiving end of that sharp intrusion, as "I would not turn over and satisfy a drunken fool that my uncle was not in bed behind me and I felt that if I had the strength of a Samson I would annihilate every one of them." Samuel Lount was captured, jailed, convicted and hanged.

And so Big Bay Point saw more than its share of Upper Canada's historic events. But none of these dire happenings were on the minds of the lucky vacationers who came to one of the two fine hotels thriving at the Point in the late 1880s. The first was Robinson House, the establishment built by farmer-cum-hotelier Isaac Robinson. It was a grand building designed to serve its guests, who could reach the hotel by one of the lake's idiosyncratic steamers and land at the Robinson wharf. The more aristocratic of the two inns was the Peninsular Park Hotel, set on 40 acres in the park of the same name. (For some time most of Big Bay Point was owned by the Peninsular Park Syndicate.) This splendid hostelry was surrounded by a spacious verandah so that the guests who occupied its sixty rooms could stroll before eating in the large dining room. Many of these guests were Americans who had come to have a taste of life in what they called the "Wilds of Canada."

Most of the shares of the Peninsular Park Syndicate were owned by F. H. Gooch, the most prominent landholder on the Point. Lake frontage was going in those days for a dollar a foot, and Gooch built his cottage, Cedarwyld, there in 1913. And he sold the point itself, a prime piece of property with a proprietary view of the lake, to a Baltimore resident, John Edward Murray. The location of Murray's purchase was a fine one. The land, however, was mostly marsh. He built his house, Land's End, in 1930 and then set about tackling his swamp. Flora Murray Wallace, Edward's granddaughter, recalls that "Draining the water from the marshy land in front of the house was a major challenge. Several methods were tried. Dredges proved unequal to the task. Finally trucks were employed to transport innumerable loads of sand to fill in the swampy area [reportedly 3,500 loads]. When this was accomplished, dirt and topsoil were driven in to cover the sand. Ultimately a beautiful front lawn was developed, surrounded by majestic trees and rugged rocks at the edges of the bay and lake." The area adjacent to the point is still a sought-after location.

In 1924, Big Bay Point acquired what became its focal point: "From early in the morning until long after the sun has marked the day's end, the golf course is dotted with players. Work on the course was started last year under the direction of Frank Thompson, son-in-law of F. H. Gooch, and member of a family of famous golfers. At that time five holes were built on what was formerly the Elliott farm. This year additional land was secured from Geo. Leslie, and another four holes added…. Judge Lennox is president of the club and F. H. Gooch is the vice-president…. The ladies have also organized with Mrs. F. H. Gooch as president and Mrs. W. E. Pepall as captain."

The course was laid out with the help of Stanley Thompson, whose brother, Frank, was married to Mildred Gooch. Stanley was golf architect of some of the leading classic golf courses in Canada, including the courses at the Banff Springs Hotel and Jasper Park Lodge as well as the Highlands Links in Cape Breton, Capilano Golf and Country Club in West Vancouver, and St. George's Golf and Country Club in Toronto. Shares were sold for fifty dollars. The course, formerly a grazing farm owned by the Pepall family, initially had a few encumbrances — rocks and groundhogs. The former were removed by "slave labour" in the form of the some of the keener prospective members, the latter by a local dog, Mickey, who chased them by the hundreds, flipped and killed them and laid them proudly on his owner's verandah.

The crowds at Big Bay Point's focal point, its golf club. The course was laid out with the advice of legendary designer Stanley Thompson.

Flora's memories from the 1930s and 1940s are of crystal-clear drinking water straight from the lake, blocks of ice carried in large tongs into the kitchen ice-box, the one public telephone in the general store, where everyone could hear your conversation, dancing to Benny Goodman, Tommy and Jimmy Dorsey, and Glenn Miller. And there were memories still vital today — carefree summers, icy swims, corn roasts, wonderful friends, plus that eternal talking point of Lake Simcoe, truly glorious sunsets. Flora Murray Wallace recalls:

Virtually everyone played golf, young, middle-aged and elderly…. The ninth tee was a good place to stop and eat raspberries growing from a nearby cluster of bushes. For many years Oscar Waghorne was the pro and his wife, Lenore, operated the canteen. Big Bay Point was a great partying community — after all, this was a vacation resort. There were three dances at the clubhouse — opening, mid-season and closing — and they were very special occasions. The ladies wore formal, floor-length dresses and the gentlemen were in commensurate attire. Weekly tea parties took place at the clubhouse, and a rotating group of ladies provided tea, dainty sandwiches, cookies and little cakes. Daughters of the hostesses served refreshments to club members and their guests who were seated in a large circle.

Cedarwyld, at Big Bay Point, in 1914

Cottage life was a new experiment and Lake Simcoe was becoming a more attractive destination due to the possibility of getting there in the family car, that exciting but unpredictable means of transportation. There is ample evidence in old diaries and guest books of the determination it took to get there, the rewards and the work that began on arrival, the number of guests and the length of time they stayed. Over the years, Cedarwyld, the summer home of Frederick Herbert and Augusta Alexandra Gooch, as with other country retreats, was a haven from the travails of town and unexpected crises — one of which, in this case, was the 1937 polio epidemic. A well-known name that appears in the guest book in August 1916 is that of Dr. Norman Bethune, a family friend.

The guest book begins, as did life at Cedarwyld, in 1914.

The season at Cedarwyld opened with a flying visit in the early days of April when the bay was found still locked and solid with ice. The shore, however, was far from being in the same condition, as we discovered to our sorrow, for after two hours of fruitless struggle, there was nothing to it but to fall back upon the good old horse to extricate the "Wolseley" from the bottomless mud. Another trip in the car was made on May 3rd when a break in the steering-gear necessitated a slow and disagreeable trip home.

By the 24th May, summer had at last driven away the chill of winter and it was a very happy and jolly party — 21 in all — that came to christen the new cottage. The house-party lasted about a week, during which time a trip was made to Jackson's Point in the "Curlew." Some excitement was caused by the "Overland" catching fire near Bradford.

Early in June the summer season was opened in earnest; but the usual lazy life of the summer cottage was not the life of Big Bay Point. Mrs. Gooch busied herself digging stones from her garden plot and piling them in walls bordering the path to the gate, while the men found plenty to keep them occupied in getting walks laid out, the pier completed, break-water walls built, and trees and underbrush cleared out and burnt.

In May 1926, golf architect Stanley Thompson came to see the new Big Bay Point golf course.

Mr. and Mrs. Stanley Thompson motored up in Willy's "Knight". Still snow in places and gravel bad on road from Churchill on. Only a few daffodils in flower. Stan walked over the course and gave instructions about what to do…. On way home there was a stop this side of New Market — the road had caved in and was in a very bad condition — had to go over ruts with mud up to the middle of car, arrived here about nine.

The summer of 1937 was a lively one. The Club House dances were a great success. Once a week the little children were amused at the Club House, ten cents being the admission fee. On account of the Polio epidemic quite a number of children stayed at the Point longer.

On departure, one satisfied guest summed up what cottage life was beginning to mean. "Left Paradise….feeling much better for the change."

Ice house at Bell Ewart under construction.

Bell Ewart: Ice Harvesting

In the days before electric refrigeration, horse-drawn wagons on delivery, loaded with straw-packed block ice, were a familiar sight. Much of that ice came from Lake Simcoe. Throughout North America it was considered the best — twelve to twenty inches thick and absolutely pure. The reasons varied but it was taken as fact that the water in the lake contained no impurities whatsoever. One winter in the 1880s, according to historian Fred Grant's recollections, "due to some freak of nature, Lake Simcoe seemed to be the only sizeable body of fresh water in North America to become frozen into commercial domestic ice, as artificial ice had not been discovered at that time." This created an unprecedented sales boom in block ice. Some was kept for use in local communities or in Toronto, but most was shipped throughout Canada and the United States — to Cincinnati, Chicago, Pittsburgh, Detroit and beyond.

At the peak of the ice-harvesting business there were at least three large companies operating in the area — the Belle Ewart Company (the company added the "e" to the town's name to give it style), the Lake Simcoe Ice Company (formerly Spring Water Ice, its new name capitalizing on the lake's reputation for purity), and the Knickerbocker Ice Company. There were also small operators in the business. These companies had locations in Kempenfeldt Bay at Barrie, at Jackson's Point, at Bell Ewart and at any place where there was land and some transportation. There were American ice companies cutting ice and sending it to cities in the eastern United States.

Hundreds of men found work on the ice. Originally the blocks were all sawed by hand until the advent of ice-harvesting machines with huge blades that were powered by automobile engines. "Talk about an industrial hazard," says Joe Fossey, boating aficionado in Barrie. "Not only could they fall into the hole but if the saw ran wild it could kill you in a minute." Farmers came with their horses and sleighs to score the blocks, cut them with toothed ploughs, and haul them out. An open water trench was left in the lake to act as a shipping canal. Stored in hay, these blocks, weighing 300 pounds, some over twenty inches thick, were kept in houses that held up to 50,000 tons of ice.

Bell Ewart was a town built on lumbering, tourism and the ice harvest. In the mid-nineteenth century when the window of prosperity opened wide, Bell Ewart was in the centre of the frame. In an article in the *Barrie Northern Advance* entitled "Northward Ho," the writer describes a trip from Toronto and his first sight of Bell Ewart. It was 1854, the year after the town had been named after a settler, James Bell Ewart, the naming ceremony presided over by a banker with American lumbering interests who had joined in the celebration.

Where is Bell Ewart? says some old traveller, who formerly travelled up Yonge Street to the Landing by stage to take the old Beaver to Barrie. But the railways have changed all that. Bell Ewart is a brand new place.... Look around and what do you see? The Bell Ewart Hotel of two stories and attic neatly painted in blue and white with stable and appurtenances there unto appertaining…. But look a little closer through the trees and you will see a great frame being made, of massive timber and several other little frames around it. That is a sawmill being erected by an American firm who propose to use fifty saws…. There is a wharf too…. Lots are now for sale at high prices. Land near the station is worth so much a foot. Village lots and parks lots, and squares are all laid out, and we have no doubt are selling freely…. In a year what change there will be on Bell Ewart; in five years how much greater will [be] the alteration!

The railroad had made it all possible. The section to Bell Ewart and Lefroy was built after the line was opened to Bradford. It was clear that a spur line to these two small settlements would provide a link to the lake on the west side. The opportunity looked golden. And the dream came true. Soon there were icehouses, steam-powered sawmills, shipping wharves, steamboat docks, a smith's shop, hotels, and stores. As planned, the rail lines carried exports of lumber and ice from the lake and brought scores of eager tourists to board one of the two steamers built there. But by the turn of the century, electric refrigeration had called a halt to the ice boom, and the other boom, in logging, had passed. The window closed on the town. It returned to its sleepy state — the boom now a memory.

Alvin and Lorne Wice loading ice.

Bell Ewart ice house.
50,000 tons of ice could be stored here.

De Grassi Point

They are located on the site of the first native encampment north of Holland Landing, that of Mississauga leader Canise, who is buried there in the Indian Mound. They live surrounded by an oak grove of such density that an early map identified the locale as Oakland. They are two tightly knit communities that have changed little in the past century — the "north-siders" and the "south-siders." Each calls the other OSPs (Other Side of the Point). This is De Grassi Point, a dual settlement unique on Lake Simcoe. This group of cottagers, notes Ted McMurrich, a fifth-generation "north-sider," has "an intense attachment to 'the Point,' amounting to a dedication…a constant emotion experienced by inhabitants from the originals through to today's cottagers." Those originals now have sixth-generation descendants.

It all began for these families in 1889 when a syndicate of five businessmen from Toronto and Lefroy purchased what was then known as Grasses Point (the name from the tall, prairie-like grasses that were part of the Indian village) on the west side of Cook's Bay. Their plan was to develop a cottage complex, a small summer village. The five were two sets of brothers, George and W. Barclay McMurrich, and George P. and Dr. William McKay, along with John Charles McKeggie.

Most of the tightly knit community of "south-siders" look to common ancestors, Byron Edmund Walker (later Sir Edmund) and Lady Walker, who bought into the syndicate's holdings in 1890. Sir Edmund built his summer home, Broadeaves, in the year of his purchase. Over the years he continued to acquire lots until he had amassed 315 acres and nearly 3,000 feet of prime shoreline, almost exclusive ownership of the south side of the Point. The Walkers called their land Innisfree, the name from William Butler Yeats' poem, "The Lake Isle of Innisfree."

The eldest Walker daughter, Ethelwyn Walker Hunter, in 1913 on Baby Beach with the rowboat Polly.

I will arise and go now, and go to Innisfree,
And a small cabin build there,
of clay and wattles made:
Nine bean-rows will I have there,
a hive for the honey bee,
And live alone in a bee-loud glade.

Sir Edmund and Lady Walker left a singular gift to their descendants, who, on the hundredth anniversary of that purchase, numbered seven children, twenty-two grandchildren, sixty-two great-grandchildren, and ninety-four

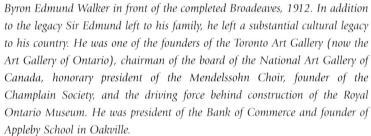

Byron Edmund Walker in front of the completed Broadeaves, 1912. In addition to the legacy Sir Edmund left to his family, he left a substantial cultural legacy to his country. He was one of the founders of the Toronto Art Gallery (now the Art Gallery of Ontario), chairman of the board of the National Art Gallery of Canada, honorary president of the Mendelssohn Choir, founder of the Champlain Society, and the driving force behind construction of the Royal Ontario Museum. He was president of the Bank of Commerce and founder of Appleby School in Oakville.

ABOVE RIGHT: *The grandchildren in 1920. Left to right: Cynthia, Bob, David, Dos, John H., Elinor, Babs, Wentworth, Alistair holding Jim, Ted, Nancy, Betty, Kitty, Alan, Lizzer, John G., Harry.*

RIGHT: *Ten years later in the obligatory Sunday dress. David, John, Bob, Harry, John G., Alan, Alistair, Ted, Wentworth, Jim.*

great-great-grandchildren. In the words of Conrad Heidenreich, one of the sixty-two, and author of the *Historical Sketch of De Grassi Point*, "Nowhere else can one find an unsubdivided cottage property the size of this one, held and operated in common [by Inisfree Limited] by so many individuals all of whom are descended from the same original owner." It is not surprising that in the reminiscences of present residents the word most often used to describe south-side De Grassi is "family." These individual cottages are part of an extended household. Their holdings are still controlled by Innisfree Farm, the private company set up by Edmund Walker in 1920 "to combine the said properties and to retain them for the use of such of his children as shall desire to occupy them." After the death of Edmund and Mary Alexander Walker's last child, Dorothy, shares were distributed to the grandchildren. Now each cottage owns shares in Innisfree Limited, which is administered by a board.

The OSP is less bound by kinship but has a similar family feeling and an intense attachment to their "north side." Sixteen of the eighteen cottages there are owned by descendants of the first four to build their summer homes — George McMurrich, J. C. McKeggie, Dr. Algernon Temple, and Augustus Walker. They shared with the south side a windmill ("pipes were laid to the houses and each house provided with one tap, usually outside the kitchen in the backyard") a sewage system, a dock, and a robust open-house policy.

A De Grassi Point Commisssion was set up in 1923 for the north-siders. Not only did it deal with communal affairs such as the water supply and septic tank, proposals for hydro, and financial affairs, but there were sub-committees for tennis and golf — there was a small course on the property — and for water supply, milk supply and ice supply. There were rules. In 1931 motor cars were prohibited from using the land between the cottages and the lake, and there were to be

No, it is not Dodge City. It is De Grassi Point after the duck hunt, Labour Day weekend, September 1901. George McMurrich, seated in the centre, holding the catch, surrounded by family and friends. From the left: Harold Roberts, Dorothy Roberts, Bryce McMurrich, Gladys McMurrich, Mrs. George McMurrich, Ethel Rose, Maude Marks, Helen McMurrich, Temple McMurrich, Charlotte Jarvis, Mabel McMurrich Roberts, Alison Roberts, Eleanor Douglas, Jessie McMurrich. In the rear: Minnie McMurrich, Z. G. Lash, Arthur McMurrich.

Sunday best at De Grassi for the boat trip to
church at Roches Point.

The McKeggie cottage, built in 1889.
Sixth-generation descendants of this original north-side family love the Point today.

no firearms operating on the Point between June 15 and September 15.

The most visible sign of successful joint ownership is the Commons, a wide swath of clear land, sand beach and tennis courts by the lake. This was also once part of the small, one-club golf course that wended its way between cottages and under obstacles winter and summer. Once the Commons had waist-high grass, but it has, since the 1950s, been carefully tended and mown and has been the scene of "kite-flying, pick-up baseball games on Saturday and/or Sunday nights with prominent and always perverse umpires...hundreds of spontaneous children's games; croquet; specialized cricket matches; badminton; deck-tennis; clock golf; knocking out fly balls; touch rugby; pass and run football; frisbee-ing; church and commemorative services; bonfires and campfires...and for many years regatta prize-givings." Life at the Point has ranged from regattas with Roches Point, Orchard Beach and Eastbourne, to birdwatching, dances, theatricals and hayrides. There were white ducks and Sunday school on Sundays, with a ferry trip to Roches Point for church, and, at least once, "grown men pitching horseshoes by the light of their cars and bowling with whiskey bottles in the breezeway."

The hundredth anniversary was celebrated in 1989 by all the families of De Grassi Point. Over 450 came to commemorate a place that is still unique and for whom the memories are legion.

Holland Marsh

Across Canada and in the United States, vegetables from the Holland Marsh are proudly identified with the label "Bradford Marsh" or simply "Marsh." But what is now called "Canada's Salad Bowl" was once called by other names — "a muck bog" being one of the most flattering. The swamp, thousands of acres adjacent to the Holland River, lay at the south end of Lake Simcoe. It was nothing more than a roadblock to travel, at best a home for wild ducks, geese and partridges, a source of peat for fuel, or of marsh hay harvested by horses that wore flat, wooden-board boots to keep them from sinking into the bog. The product was used for stuffing mattresses. When, in the mid-1800s, someone suggested that the levels of Lakes Simcoe and Couchiching be lowered so that the Holland River and marsh could be drained, the outraged reaction to this suggestion put further talk on the subject to bed for fifty years.

And then, starting in 1910, two ideas came together to produce today's cornucopia. The first came from a Bradford man, David Watson, who was convinced of the potential of the rich marsh muck. He brought Professor William Day of the Ontario Agricultural College to take a look. To Professor Day the muck looked beautiful. From two to forty feet deep, it could make a massive vegetable patch. In 1912 he formed a syndicate that bought 4,000 acres of marsh. Plans to begin work had to wait until after the First World War but eventually a Holland Marsh Drainage Commission was formed. It took five years to drain the marsh and build canals and dykes, but by 1930 the area was pronounced ready for planting. However, farming this drained bog proved next to impossible. Who could manage it without special skills?

The answer was found through another man to whom the swamp looked appealing. He was John Snor, Canadian representative of the Netherlands Emigration Foundation. There were over 150,000 Dutch immigrants in Canada; many sponsored after the war by Canadian farmers. About half had settled in Ontario and were working on farms, hoping to own a farm of their own some day.

These men and women from the Netherlands had the necessary skills. To them the Holland Marsh was land like that on which they had been expert in market gardening at home, where they had farmed small muck plots on land reclaimed from the North Sea. (They might have assumed that the Holland Marsh was called after their homeland. In fact it had nothing to do with the Netherlands. Governor Simcoe had named the area and nearby river for the Surveyor-General of Canada, Major Samuel Holland.) The first seventeen families, fifteen Dutch, one German, and one English, were settled on the marsh in 1934. They were given a one-time grant of $600 per family — $450 for five acres of land, the rest for a house and living expenses for twelve months. They got through the first years of small crops with the help of the generous people of Bradford.

Year by year the crops grew larger. A settlement called Ansnorveldt was formed, seeds were obtained from Holland, co-operatives were started, advanced farming and storage methods were adopted. Now, where those booted horses gathered hay, a rich harvest is gathered, overflowing the storage sheds each fall.

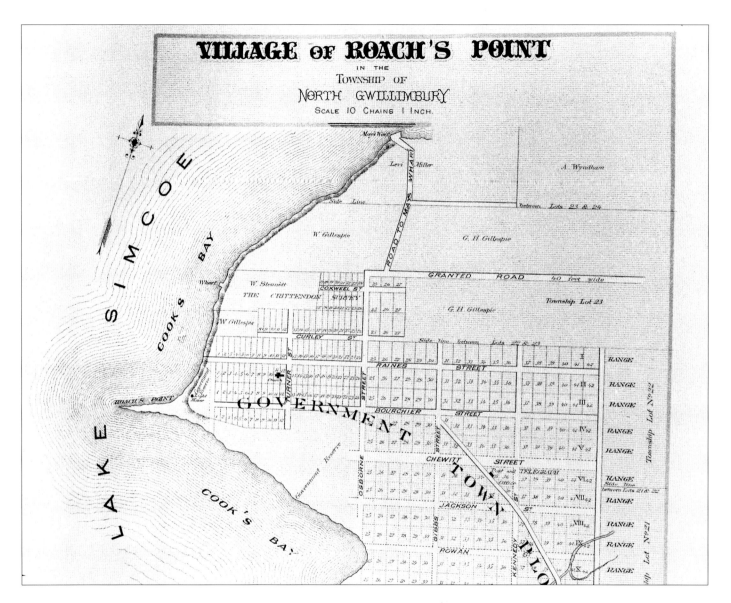

The town plan for Roches Point as capital of Upper Canada, Peregrine Maitland's "once and future" dream.

Roches Point: A Capital Place

I f it had all worked out according to plan, the tiny village of Roches Point, perched quietly on the shores of Cook's Bay, would be the hub of Ontario's wheel today.

That, at any rate, was the way it was planned in 1822 by Upper Canada's lieutenant-governor, Major General Sir Peregrine Maitland. York, the capital of Upper Canada, had been described by one visitor as "a piece of low marshy land which is better calculated as a frog-pond or beaver meadow than for the residence of human beings, [where] agues and intermittent fevers affect five-sevenths of the people." Another summed up the place succinctly as "dull, dirty and disgusting." And it was considered vulnerable. York had already been attacked by American invaders who, in 1812, burned the parliament buildings and all government records.

In 1822 Maitland purchased 200 acres at what was then called Keswick (later renamed Roches Point after the first settler, James Roche) for £450 and had the town site laid out — a government reserve, town lots, and streets named after officers from Wellington's army in the battle of Waterloo. The government reserve included a fine point of land that would have served well for Maitland's official residence. There Sir Peregrine and his wife, Lady Sarah Lennox (one of fourteen children of the prolific fourth duke of Richmond and Lennox, governor-in-chief of British North America), could have enjoyed Lake Simcoe's breathtaking sunsets and kept a lookout for Americans, should any have had the temerity to venture so far from Lake Ontario.

Roches Point was to have been at the centre of a grand plan: the chief in a chain of sixteen large towns between Lake Simcoe and the Ottawa River with interior navigation as a link; the focal point of land and water communications between Lake Simcoe and Lake Ontario and between Lake Simcoe and Georgian Bay; and the start of a road linking Lake Simcoe and the Grand River at Brantford. Its influence and power would have stretched from east to west and from north to south, touching the extremities of Ontario's boundaries and beyond. The little burg would be "on the axis of a trade route to the Canadian West." Surveys were started for connecting roads, a Trent waterway, and townships along the Trent and the Rideau. The plan received tentative approval in England from Lord Bathurst.

But it was not to be. The cost was astronomical for the times. The road from Lake Simcoe to Ottawa alone was calculated to cost over £4,400. Other plans were afoot, in particular for a Welland Canal. As well, nobody wanted to move. Maitland's enthusiasm was not shared by those officials who had recently relocated from Newark (Niagara) to muddy York. They had settled in relative comfort and, in spite of the mosquitoes and ague, wanted to stay put. But the plan stayed on the books and in the minds of some. In 1829, when Edward O'Brien of Shanty Bay stayed on the Roches Point site, he wrote that this "lovely piece of land" was well suited to be Upper Canada's capital.

So for better or worse the village lost the chance to become home to British nobility and government officials. But times were not dull at

Christ Church,
Roches Point.

Roches Point. The black sheep of the famous American Dodge family made his home there. Close to his handsome retreat is located one of the most beautiful fieldstone churches in Ontario, built by an astute and entrepreneurial pastor. Steamships landed nearby at Captain May's wharf. At one time the hamlet supported two hotels, two general stores, a butcher shop, a telephone exchange and other commercial establishments.

The Reverend Walter Stennett built Christ Church Roches Point as therapy. He had come to the village after a career as minister, teacher and principal at Toronto's Upper Canada College — a nervous breakdown was the result of life at that prestigious boys' school. He started building the church in 1862 and by its completion had recovered his health and created a building of timeless beauty. To stand in the graveyard that surrounds the exquisite fieldstone church is to be transported to an English country churchyard. And the good rector's business acumen returned with his health. He began investing in real estate, picking up some prime local sites, one of which appealed to a man with imposing credentials and a name to match — Anson Green Phelps Dodge.

Dodge, scion of that prominent American family and owner of lumber interests in Canada and the United States, pulled up stakes in 1869, leaving his wife and children and his homes in New York and on St. Simons Island, Georgia. With a singular lack of timing, he picked Christmas Eve for his departure. His father, philanthropist William Earle Dodge, paid off Anson's debts and gave him a cheque for $750,000 to expand the Canadian lumber interests. This he did, becoming president of the Georgian Bay Lumber Company and earning the title of "lumber king of the north."

Shortly thereafter, A. G. P. Dodge turned up in Roches Point, where he acquired 115 acres of property, part of which was a house and grounds purchased from Reverend Stennett for $5,000. Dodge then showed that, however unorthodox his lifestyle, he had superb taste in architecture. He turned the existing building into a gabled mansion with a verandah that hugs the house, and French doors and ornate windows that flood it with light. With his father's cheque in hand he spared no expense and hired Frederick Law Olmsted to design gardens in the 40 acres surrounding Beechcroft. Olmsted had the experience for the job. He was the leading American landscape artist of the day, having co-designed Central Park in New York with Calvert Vaux, designed Prospect Park in Brooklyn and Mount Royal Park in Montreal, and created the master plan for Niagara Falls. For Dodge's estate, Olmsted created romantic paths, arbours and bridges, with an adjacent deer park. Nearby were a number of parterres, "glowing with beautiful tints of the most choice flowers of the season," while in the conservatory was "one of the most extensive and varied displays of exotic plants and flowers in the country."

Dodge left Roches Point a legacy other than the house, becoming as notorious in his new home as he had been in his former one. Not content with a thriving lumber business in Muskoka and Georgian Bay and a vice-presidency of the Toronto, Simcoe and Muskoka Junction Railway, Dodge decided to become a Canadian citizen and enter politics. But his political career foundered for a variety of reasons, one of which was the discovery that he had forged two laudatory letters purported to be from clergy, letters that he had used in his election campaign. In one, the writer (Dodge) described the candidate (Dodge) in these glowing terms: "A man of more liberal, broad, Christian views cannot be found [who leads] an energetic, earnest life for the good of others, and noble and high aims are his life's record."

Others held different opinions. The *Newmarket Era* commented caustically that "He said he found it necessary to bury his modesty; and it could scarcely be supposed that a very deep grave would be required."

Dodge later lost Beechcroft through bankruptcy. The house was sold to Toronto businessman Walter Gillespie, who rented it as a summer residence and a school for clergy (the numbers can still be seen on the upstairs bedrooms). In 1895, Beechcroft was purchased by Toronto financier E. B. Osler and it remains in the family today.

On the neighbouring property stands a mansion of equal longevity and grandeur — and a somewhat more traditional history. From their lookout, the widow's walk on the top of the stately 1871 house called Lakehurst, the family of British naval officer and master mariner Captain Isaac May could scan the lake and pace anxiously while they

Lake steamer leaving Roches Point.

awaited his return to his home wharf. His voyages took him around Lake Simcoe as he commanded his *Emily May*, one of the steamships that plied the lake, taking passengers and their possessions from Holland Landing to their destination of choice. To pass the time while watching for Captain May, his family could admire their property, purchased in 1864 — twenty-five acres of farmland formerly owned by Alfred Wyndham, an English gentleman who had fought in the Crimean War. Their extensive gardens contained an eclectic showing of flowers, indigenous and imported, and hundreds of fruit trees. And on their lawns stood part of the tangible history of Lake Simcoe — an old fieldstone cabin that had served as a trading post for the native people of the Georgina and Snake Island reserves, and an early board-and-batten barn that pre-dated the main house. When the property was sold in 1877 it was reported to have 700 fruit trees on its 97 acres. In 1911, Lakehurst was purchased by Wilmot Deloui Matthews. It passed to his son, Arnold Clayton Matthews, then his grandson Douglas, remaining in the Matthews family for nearly ninety years.

Eastbourne Golf Club

Sheep cropped the grass at the Eastbourne Golf Club and performed other functions as well. The minutes of 1921 recorded "the desirability of the Club owning a flock of sheep to help keep the grass and weeds down and fertilize the fairways. Authority was given to go ahead and arrange to purchase if possible a flock of good sheep, thoroughbreds preferred, and erect a small shelter for them."

It was 1912 when Douglas Wood, a young boy of twelve, took a trip to the Isle of Jersey with his father. While there he tried his hand at golf. On returning to his Eastbourne home he laid out a small course on the commons near his cottage — five holes with tomato cans in each green and cricket stumps for pins. The grass was too rough for anything but short mashee shots, however, the men and women of the surrounding cottages took to the game and played along in their seven- or-eight-somes, the groups criss-crossing as they played. In 1913 they leased the land and formed the Eastbourne Golf Club, no doubt the first golf club on Lake Simcoe. Frank Freeman, at that time pro at the Rosedale Golf Club, designed the course and supervised grading and seeding. The length of the course was increased to nine holes in 1915. A charter membership in the club cost $50 and annual dues were $15. Eleven charter members joined, providing a capital of $550 to go on.

From 1918 to 1922, the Eastbourne Golf Club made the *Mail and Empire* on an annual basis for a series of exhibition matches held to benefit the Red Cross. The matches attracted media attention due to the calibre of the participants — George Cummings of the Toronto Golf Club and

B. L. Anderson, secretary of the Royal Canadian Golf Association took on George S. Lyon, eight times Canadian champion, and Willie Freeman of Lambton. The paper described the play of the foursome as ranging from outstanding to brilliant, with the occasional "foozled" shot. As for the course it was "still a little rough in spots, but [it] is very quaint and provides almost endless opportunities for the enthusiasts who frequent the popular watering place. It is inclined to be flat, but with the addition of some more bunkers and traps…Eastbourne should prove to be one of the most attractive courses in Canada." Improvements had been made by the next year and the course was called "a very sporty links" and in good condition. No doubt some credit for this should go to the sheep for doing a job of eating and fertilizing.

Ladies Field Day, Eastbourne Golf Club, 1954.

Orchard Beach

Celebrities could sometimes be seen on the nearby Orchard Beach Golf Course. Conn Smythe, founder of Maple Leaf Gardens, owner of the Toronto Maple Leafs, and himself a celebrity, had a summer residence there. Along with Kenneth Smith and others in the neighborhood, he established the Orchard Beach Golf Club in 1926. Another summer resident, Mr. Ross, then general manager of the Canadian National Exhibition, brought some of the show's stars who wanted a game of golf up to Lake Simcoe. Such celebrities as Bob Hope visited there. Here Conn Smythe, at left, is seen with Danny Kaye.

Conn Smythe with hockey greats Ted Kennedy, "Hap" Day and Eddie Shore in 1950.

Ladies in their finery for an IODE meeting, Laura Secord Chapter.
Miss Bessie Sibbald, centre, with the best hat.

The Holland Landing band visits Jackson's Point for July 1st celebrations.

Jackson's Point in its Sunday best.

The ice house and mill, Jackson's Point.

M ajor William Kingdom Rains was a man of many parts. Commissioned lieutenant at sixteen, he fought under the Duke of Wellington in the Napoleonic Wars, became a close personal friend of Lord Byron, was made a Knight of the Cross of the Imperial Order of St. Leopold and, while not engaged with the enemy, enjoyed a reputation as a "jovial gentleman, notorious for his success with the fair sex." (He was seemingly reluctant to give up these successful amorous pursuits. The journal entry on his wedding day reads "Married and be d-----d to it 15th August 1811.")

Rains, a man with an eye for beauty, was one of the first of many retired military officers to discover the undulating curves of nature in that stretch of Lake Simcoe's shore from Roches Point through Jackson's Point and on to Pefferlaw. He purchased a log house overlooking the lake. A journal entry for May 6, 1830, noted "Embarked for Canada...at Lake Simcoe 14th July...took up residence at Penrains 4th October 1830." The house, called Penn Rains or Sutton Lodge, was named after the estate Rains had built for his family in Pembrokeshire, England. There his wife patiently awaited his return from the wars or his colonial travels, visits that resulted in the birth of eleven children in twenty-three years.

Rains, however, was not lonely on the isolated shores of the lake, nor, seemingly, had he given up his amorous pursuits. Living with him were two beautiful sisters whom he had persuaded to accompany him on this adventure to share his home and affections. The trio was compatible enough to live there for five years, though Rains clearly made enough trips back to England to account for the birth of three more children during that time. Rains and his ladies left in 1835, the ending to their unusual story somewhat of a mystery.

But the woman who bought Penn Rains was no mystery. She was a product of her era, a forthright Victorian lady who had received a disturbing report — that her son William, who had settled in Orillia along with his brother Charles, presumably to learn farming, had been living in a tavern and engaging in "shocking" activities. Leaving her ailing husband and crossing the Atlantic alone to visit the colonies was not too much trouble if she could satisfy herself about the state of the boys' morals. The lady was Susan Sibbald. Whatever her sons' activities were, they must have passed muster, for this doughty and decisive lady took the time to tour Lake Simcoe. She fell in love with the same stretch of lakeshore that had enticed Major Rains and bought his house and 500 acres of land.

By this time it was mid-winter, an unsuitable time for an Atlantic crossing, and so Susan, then fifty-nine, spent three months in a bitterly cold log house, worried about her ailing husband and disturbed that there was a tavern on her property and no church in the neighbourhood.

Nothing had prepared her for this. Raised in England in a home where the arts were part of life and Sir Walter Scott a visitor, educated in a chic school in Bath, Susan came out in London society, enjoyed a whirlwind season, then moved to Scotland where her father was building his estate, Eildon Hall. There she met and married Colonel

William Sibbald. The couple had eleven children. While their brood increased, however, the family fortune decreased as Sibbald, retired from the army, made unsuccessful efforts at farming. Fortunately, as author Marian Fowler notes in her *Portrait of Susan Sibbald: Writer and Pioneer*, the young debutante was "gifted with an irrepressible optimism towards life and a predisposition towards contentment." She needed it.

On her return to Scotland in the spring of 1836, Susan found that her husband had died in her absence — word had never reached her in far-off Lake Simcoe. And so, accompanied by her three youngest sons, ages thirteen, twelve and eight, she crossed the Atlantic with the family grandfather clock, dining-room table, and other treasures large and small. The party made their way up to Holland Landing and across the lake by steamer. Susan began immediately to re-create her Scottish home, calling the log house Eildon Hall. A two-storey addition created a white-walled Regency cottage surrounded by a verandah. It was soon filled with all the comforts and luxuries of the day. The world was back in its appropriate orbit with croquet on the lawn followed by tea, and with music, dancing, and all the delight and sparkle young people could provide for evening soirées. And in everything the unwavering standard for behaviour, lifestyle and amenities was unquestionably to be found in the British Isles. The family was always proud to quote the remark made by Stephen Leacock, who had grown up in nearby Egypt: "Most notable of all these southern settlements was Eildon Hall, the family home of the Sibbalds....in beauty unsurpassed." The estate remained in the Sibbald family until 1957 when the Provincial Government acquired the building and opened it to the public.

Susan Sibbald's Eildon Hall was an integral part of what became an aristocratic society existing on the rugged shores of this deeply forested lake. The settlers, emigrants of the British upper class, were determined to re-create the life they had left behind in the British Isles. They built wilderness manors in the colonies, with manor house, barns and outbuildings, and enough servants to ensure their comfort. To complete the picture, they each imported a well-loved name for their new home.

Miss Meta Patterson, Miss Carrie Bourchier, Mrs. Nellie (Bourchier) Patterson, and her brother, John Bourchier, in front of the Manor, Sutton, built in 1845 by James Bourchier. John Bourchier married into the Anderson family. His brother-in-law, James Anderson, husband of Susannah Bourchier, developed the first cottage complex at Jackson's Point. It was called the Pinery. James was the son of James Anderson, chief factor of the Hudson's Bay Company, and the grandson of Robert Anderson, pioneer in Sutton. The Anderson family was also related to Sir Alexander Mackenzie, the great explorer, after whom the Mackenzie River was named. He followed it from Lake Athabasca to the Arctic in 1789.

Before Major Rains had set up his love-nest, and before Susan Sibbald had crossed the Atlantic to check on the habits of her offspring, another family, one with roots in tenth-century France, had come to the area. They were to be instrumental in establishing a permanent, self-supporting settlement on the shores of the Black River. Their name was Bourchier.

Captain William Bourchier was sent to Penetanguishene in 1812 to supervise construction of a battleship of which he was to have command. For this operation an anchor was hauled by fifty yoke of oxen from York up to Holland Landing — the war ended and so did the anchor's journey. William was granted 2,000 acres of land and persuaded his brother James to settle on Lake Simcoe in 1818.

William and James Bourchier could boast a family tree transplanted to England with the Norman Conquest. Its branches were laden with notables — a crusader with Richard I, an Archbishop of Canterbury, the wife of Oliver Cromwell. (The text printed on the back of an old portrait of Cromwell still in the family's possession notes that the bride "may not have much character, but her husband never ceased to love her," and thirty years after their marriage he writes to her "Truly, if I love not too well, I think I err not on the other hand much. Thou art dearer to me than any creature; let that suffice.")

William Bourchier married Amelia Jackson, daughter of John Mills Jackson, after whom Jackson's Point was named, and the newly married couple left for India where they remained until Amelia died in 1837. James Bourchier, one of the first permanent settlers in Georgina Township, almost single-handedly founded and ran a town near Jackson's Point. He became justice of the peace, postmaster and miller, and built saw and grist mills, a cheese factory, a woollen mill, and a general store that opened onto the Black River and was easily accessible to those who travelled by this meandering route. He made

sure that there were churches in the village that grew up around his mill. St. James' Anglican Church was built in 1857 — James gave the land and raised money in England in order for this structure to arise. In 1845, Bourchier built his manor house, which was called simply the Manor. It still stands, in excellent condition, beside his mill. The community he founded is Sutton.

After the death of his wife, William came back to Sutton, remarried, and in 1840 built his own manor house nearby. He called it The Briars, not after a home of his own, but after a house owned by friends that had served as a prison for Napoleon before he was sent to St. Helena. Bourchier's Briars was a stucco building in the Georgian style with a large, welcoming front door covered by a distinguished portico and flanked by imposing windows on the main level. In the 1870s The Briars was sold to Frank Sibbald. He added two wings, which tripled the size of the house, and built a fine carriage house. But he needed more. His collection of imported peacocks had no home and so he built an ornate octagonal building with a window and door on each of the eight sides, adding something unique to this elite strip of lakeshore. The Briars has remained in the Sibbald family to this day. When Bessie Sibbald, Frank's niece, inherited the property, she built cottages along the shore. Jack Sibbald, her nephew, next in line, established The Briars Country Club, incorporated these cottages, made extensive changes and opened it to guests, offering them wartime ration-ticket menus, bridge, golf, and rooms with a shared bath. His son John turned The Briars into an all-season resort. It is one of the finest in Canada.

Along the lakeshore, east of the Black River, is a prime spot from which to enjoy the lake today. Mossington Park is named after Thomas Mossington, another retired naval officer who chose this popular section of lakeshore as home. Having first seen this part of

A gathering at The Briars.

Lee Farm, the home of pioneer Captain Simon Lee. Recently retired from the East India Company, Captain Lee and his wife, Martha Ready Smith, settled first in Thornhill and then, in 1835, located on 500 acres at the eastern end of the Sibbald land adjacent to what is now Sibbald Park. There Lee farmed and built his two-storey frame house, which still stands today. He was much involved in the task of raising money for a church in the settlement. The result of his efforts and those of others was the beautiful St. George's Church. The Lees had twelve children, including one who was stillborn and twins who died as infants.

Lake Simcoe when he spent two years timber-cruising, selecting timber to be used as masts for the British navy, Mossington returned on his retirement and built an imposing home using stucco, which had become popular as a sturdy exterior providing good insulation. He called his new home Plumstead, another import from England. In retirement he began a new career as a magistrate, using the dining room of his house as a courtroom, and allowed a school to be opened in another part of his house. And in his retirement he took a new wife, a young woman of twenty-one. This prompted a number of the locals to treat old Thomas and his young bride to a Canadian custom — a shivaree. They serenaded the couple on their wedding night with a cacophony of cowbells, sleigh bells and everything else that made an infernal noise until the frustrated groom bribed them to go away to the local tavern.

At the east end of the Sibbald property, Captain Simon Lee, who had just retired from service with the East India Company, bought 500 acres of land and built Lee Farm, a two-storey frame house where he settled his wife and daughters. Mrs. Lee was a woman who, like the neighbouring women of her class, knew the proper way in which things should transpire, particularly when it came to the marriages of her daughters. There were three girls and three suitors. They should, she knew, sort themselves out in order of age — the eldest to marry the eldest and so on. The suitors, particularly William Sibbald, had other ideas. He, the eldest suitor, had chosen the second daughter. This would not do. He must marry the first girl. And he did, with the help of an ample allowance of brandy on his wedding day, but the mother-in-law was right and the marriage proved to be an exceedingly happy one.

And so this group, enjoying each other's company socially, and generally of like mind, had established a bit of the Old Country on Lake Simcoe. But one essential thing was lacking — a church. They lost no time. John Mills Jackson initiated the plans. Susan Sibbald and John Comer gave land for the church and parsonage. (A regimental sergeant-major with a distinguished military career, Comer was one of the two original Crown grantees, along with Captain Bourchier.) Thomas Mossington designed the building, first creating a wooden model. And James and William Bourchier had 15,000 feet of timber transported to the site. A group of volunteers came for the church-raising bee and the church was completed by 1839.

Forty years later the first St. George's church was replaced by the stone building now on the site. Its stands adjacent to Sibbald Memorial Park, so well known to campers today, and was dedicated in memory of Susan Sibbald by her sons. Retired naval officer Captain Thomas Sibbald supervised the construction proceedings in Glengarry

cap with ribbons flowing down the back. All was done according to naval tradition with a rum ration at "eight bells" each working day and a toast to Queen Victoria. Governor Simcoe made a significant contribution, donating the east window of the church, which was designed and worked by his seven daughters. It draws visitors today, as do the graves of two Canadian authors who achieved international fame. The grave site of Mazo de La Roche, whose Jalna books were the rage of the day, is marked with a Celtic cross. And humorist and Lake Simcoe eulogist Stephen Leacock is buried here under a weeping mountain ash tree in surroundings about which he wrote. "The church, the graveyard, and beyond it the sweep of land that runs down to Eildon Hall and the lake, with a background of bay and island, a forest sunk in the waters, — possesses a wistful loneliness that no artificial beauty of the landscape gardener can emulate or approach."

By the turn of the century, tourists and cottagers had discovered the charms of this part of Lake Simcoe, as had those first urbane settlers. There was a need for transportation from Toronto north for the ever-increasing numbers who wanted to make the trip. First a branch of the main line from Mount Albert stopped at Sutton and, by 1907, the Toronto and York Radial Railway reached Jackson's Point. It was part of a system including 137 miles of track around Toronto, the longest section of which linked the city and Lake Simcoe. One of the first commuter lines and the ultimate in transportation for its time, it was electrified in 1890, completed to Newmarket by 1899, and extended in a "high-speed" right of way to Sutton by 1909. For fifty years it provided smooth transportation north from the city, the like of which has not been seen since.

An astonishing five trips a day were available on the line between Toronto and Newmarket, which then boasted a population of two thousand. From Newmarket the line wended its way north through

Jackson's Point — not a one-horse town.

The old reliable Radial car at Sutton.

attempted to accommodate the destinations of all its customers, stopping every couple of miles. Traces of the system still exist, including Metro Road, which runs along part of the original path, and the Radial station in Sutton, the last stop on the line.

Scores of passengers disembarked in Sutton — women in their important hats, men with their bowlers and canes — to be met by the carriages that crowded in to take them to one of the many hotels in town. Passengers could stroll along Sutton's High Street past the Town Hall where the Sutton Band played on the balcony as well as for dances, then past five hotels and numerous blacksmiths shops, liveries, a millinery shop where tea was served with each purchase, small department stores, a bakery and a shoe manufacturing shop. (This was a more pleasant stroll after the council outlawed spitting on the streets and passed a bylaw against speeding horses.) Tourists could meander through the fine residential section of town or leave directly to dress for high tea at The Briars.

Sharon and Queensville on into Keswick, then veered slightly west to follow the lake through Roches Point and Eastbourne and on to Jackson's Point, finally curving down into Sutton. The Sutton stop was the hundredth on the two-and-three-quarter-hours trip as the line

The Enterprise *docks at Jackson's Point.*
The wharf was used for the overflow crowd from Levi Miller's Jackson's Point Hotel.

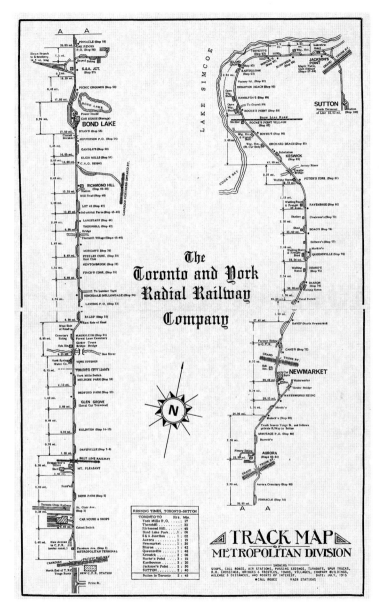

The Radial stop in Jackson's Point was equally busy. A stay at elegant Lakeview House could be had for six dollars a week for adults, three dollars a week for children. There were many other hotels, and entertainment in "genteel restaurants," dance halls and casinos, as well as all the amenities offered by the lake itself. A favourite pastime with the children was to put a penny on the track and see it flattened when the Radial had gone through. Jackson's Point was the site of many ice houses, filled with twenty-five- to fifty-pound blocks of ice that had been cut from the lake in winter and packed in sawdust. If the day was hot and the proprietor of the ice house in a good mood there might be a chance for the ultimate treat — a hunk of ice cut off for a cooling chew.

Beaverton

It was on Christmas Eve, 1870, that the first train pulled into Beaverton. After that momentous event, passengers, taken right to the dock where a lake steamer waited, could set out directly for Thorah Island, two miles away, venture on to Orillia, Lake Couchiching and the much-travelled Severn River route to Georgian Bay, or take a short excursion to Strawberry Island, known locally as the best spot to catch black bass in the two lakes. It was a proud day for this harbour, acknowledged in the area as the most important on the lake.

It would be another twenty years before Beaverton's harbour received official designation as a port, but that was only a formality. Where the Beaver River entered the lake there had long been a stopping place for sailing vessels, lake steamers and the later screw-propeller ships. And there had always been activity in the harbour — the scene of departures for special excursions such as the trip on the *Kendrick* to Orillia for the eagerly anticipated 1832 championship race between Jake Gaudaur and Ned Hanlan, or for one of the romantic moonlight cruises. There were derbies of all kinds, including log rolling. And there were regattas. One brought raves from the *Barrie Northern Advance* on September 26, 1889: "Last

Sailboat in Beaverton harbour.

Monday there was a regatta at Beaverton and a number of Barrie yachts went across to take part.... Mr. Levi Carley ran from here to Beaverton with the *Jewel* in four hours — the wind was stiff and the water very rough but the *Jewel* proved herself a first class boat for her class. The Beaverton people were astonished that the trip across the lake could be made by such a boat as the *Jewel* in such a sea."

In early days, before there was any docking facility, sailing vessels had to anchor offshore while their long-suffering passengers took to a small boat and rowed in. Then a pier was built, hotels appeared and, in 1891, work started for a grand port at a new site. By 1912 there was an impressive south pier of cement, its long walkway and iron railings extending 1,200 feet into the lake. This new harbour took shape in an ideal location, a deep slit in from the lake with protecting wings in the form of two long piers, each with a lighthouse at the point. Tall sailboat houses were built, a sight long familiar and one distinguishing the port. (They were two-storey buildings, with the upper floor a potential residence.) Five years after the work was completed the *Beaverton Express* proudly announced that the government had spent $11,000 on the harbour, a sizeable amount for the time.

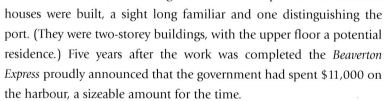

As well as the eagerly awaited arrival of the lake steamers, the Beaverton harbour had accommodated regular trips of the small but essential private ferries that plied their way back and forth from Thorah Island. The old stalwart, the *Belle of Thorah,* was succeeded by the *Thorah Belle,* a multipurpose vessel with an imaginative owner. When her days carrying passengers and mail back and forth between island and mainland came to an end, her captain, Thomas Warren Jr., simply cut off the stern, put a door in the opening, stood her on end, and turned her into a post office. The *Thorah Belle* served well in that capacity, only occasionally having to deal with a prankster such as the one who slipped a rooster in the door and waited to see the results — the mail was a bit discoloured that day.

Recently Jim White, great-great-grandson of a Beaverton pioneer, stood by White's Creek, a quiet stream shaded by willows and opening to the lake. The creek, he explained, was named for his ancestor, John Edward White, surveyor of Thorah Township. John's son, James, and his wife, Jeanette Waddell, found good farmland on Thorah Island and became two of the first settlers there. Others followed, including four Toronto men who established a campsite. Since 1892 they and their descendants have come to the "Camp Ground." Much of Thorah Island was a Chippewa reserve, pasture land and fishing grounds, but over the years a large part of that land has been sold and subdivided.

The past is still visible in Beaverton, in the brick house, log house and jail restored by the historical society, and in the old stone Presbyterian church that dates from 1840. There is no better way to get a sense of the atmosphere of the town in the 1800s than to hear some of the names of the pioneers who gathered there — McMillan, Bruce, Fraser, McCuiag, Campbell, Calder, Gordon, McLachlan,

The Thorah Belle *in her glory days, before she became the post office.*

McFadyen, McDougall, Stewart, McKay, Cameron, McRae, McDonald, McPherson, McEwen, McTaggart and more. Beaverton was Scottish. Yes, there was the occasional Irishman and some English, but the majority by 1842 were overwhelming from Scotland. And they were stalwart, as their stories tell. One hardy Scot, James Gordon, the town's first blacksmith, transported his family and belongings up the length of Lake Simcoe from Holland Landing to Beaverton, steadfastly rowing his small boat the gruelling distance. Another favourite tale is that of the Scot who was walking home with his heavy bag of flour slung over his shoulder. A traveller on horseback stopped to say that he could take man but not flour, as his horse could not support that load. "You give me a ride," said the Scot, "and I'll carry the flour on my shoulder."

The Trent Canal

It took eighty-seven years to build — from 1833 to 1920 — but when completed the Trent-Severn Waterway joined Lake Huron via Georgian Bay to the Bay of Quinte, a distance of 386 kilometres. Nine locks and a marine railway take traffic from the Severn River to Kirkfield at Lake Simcoe — an 80-metre lift. The section from there to Lake Ontario is comprised of thirty-three locks through the Kawartha lakes and the Otonobee and Trent Rivers with the Lindsay lock and the Murray Canal making connections to Lake Scugog and Lake Ontario respectively.

Surveyors first set the course of the waterway, using existing rivers and determining where dredging could deepen the waterway and where blasting would be necessary. Then crews undertook the dangerous blasting process, excavations for the locks were dug, concrete was poured, and 125 dams were built to control and regulate water levels in the Trent and Severn watersheds. From its early days the waterway was a channel to move logs that had been hewn in the lumber camps in the winter months and stored at waters' edge waiting for the break-up. Mills were located beside the dams' powerful waters. Steamboats, tugs and working vessels travelled the calm waters of the canals. The Trent was a dependable road.

The men who built the canal, the locks, including two massive lift-locks at Peterborough and Kirkfield, the swing bridges, marine railways, and dams were mainly recent immigrants who worked for low wages, lived in poor accommodation, and endured hazardous conditions. A preponderance were Irish. In *"I Remember...,"* An Oral History of the Trent-Severn Waterway, the words of some of those men from interviews by the author, Daniel Francis, re-create the times.

About the dynamiting: "They'd blow the whistle to warn everybody that they were going to blast and everybody would run for cover and it was quite common that a big piece of rock would fly over and come through your front verandah or smash the roof of the house or something. They always paid, but it wasn't a very comfortable feeling sitting in the house never knowing what was coming in."

Living conditions: "were absolutely nothing but single plywood shacks that were covered with tar paper and in a couple or three cases, why they had a platform made there on the ground, or the rocks rather, and had tents over them, even in winter."

"They put two double beds in each room and when I went in there first, there was as many as six men sleeping in one room. Two fellows in a bed sleep in there for the night and they'd get up and go to work at 8 o'clock in the morning and the fellows at 8 o'clock in the morning go back, climb in that bed and sleep in there till they got up. The beds were always in use. They never got cooled off.

The life: "We had our bunkhouse and the cookhouse and well, then you made our own entertainment more or less. Some guys would have a fiddle in there and mouth organ and stuff like that or you got some of these old timers that had done a lot of time in the woods, they were great story tellers and you got quite some real tall stories ."

*Modern-day view
of the historic Trent Canal.*

The divers who made repairs: "And we went down there one morning and I'd say it must have been, oh it was over 20 below, and I went down…I just got out of the water and Bob took me and set me down and he couldn't undo my laces. They were froze. So he tried to undo my helmet and he couldn't undo my helmet and there I am, fully dressed….and I couldn't get in the cab….So the four of them picked me up, threw me on the back of the truck and I laid on the back of the truck and they brought me right through town to the shop and they stood me up there in the corner and I stood there until I thawed out…."

An invaluable link in the early days, a way for farmers, loggers, lumber barons and merchants to move their considerable wares, the waterway was conceived with great expectations. It was to be the major commercial highway of the future. But the logging and steamboat period was replaced by the era of railways and huge freighters. Within decades there was talk of closing the waterway down. Once again expectations proved incorrect.

Where shipping had fallen off, the family boat took over — and took over by the thousands, filling the water-roadway with fleets of recreational craft. Now a week's trip takes captain and crew through thirty-six conventional locks, two flight locks, two hydraulic lift-locks and a marine railway. En route the Kirkfield Lift Lock, which can take 1,500 tonnes at each end, easily hoists each vessel nearly 50 feet in the air. The canal of post-Confederation Ontario has become a heritage route today.

The Chippewa and the Islands

Snake, Fox, Georgina and Thorah

The land was strategic. The government wanted it. And they got it. After the War of 1812, the chiefs, Snake, Aisance, and Yellowhead, surrendered almost two million acres around Lakes Simcoe and Couchiching to the government. They got £4,000 for the first surrender, in 1815, and £1,200 in goods for the second, three years later. It was land that made up what are now the counties of Simcoe, Grey, Wellington, and Dufferin. It was land with a long history for its native people.

Champlain first came to the area between Georgian Bay and Kempenfeldt Bay in 1615. It was Huron territory and he was awestruck by the fertility and beauty of the country. In keeping with his promise to lead a secret attack into the Iroquois stronghold, he set out from Cahiagué, at the Narrows, with a war party of Huron and French. They were headed south of Lake Ontario to Upper New York State. Repulsed, the party returned to their homes. Years later, decimated by European disease, the Huron were easy prey for the Iroquois who invaded their territory. But this acquisition was only temporary. The Ojibwa came from Lake Superior, and by the end of the seventeenth century, these lands, indeed the lands in nearly all of Southern Ontario, were Chippewa domain.

Chief Charles Big Canoe.

The colonial government had plans for this terrain. It was desirable and had military importance as an inland route. But the loyalty of the native people was essential. The policy of the British government became one of keeping the Chippewa loyal and divided, and of acquiring their lands. And so they were told that the King would look after them. He would, according to former Ojibwa chief H. A. McCue, protect them, and "manage all their property, provide victuals, clothes and lodgings, protect their rights and redress any wrongs." In return they would support him and fight for him if necessary. Then at the end of the War of 1812 the colonial government, with officers to reward and loyal settlers to secure with grants, intensified its efforts to get their land. This resulted in the surrender of the two million acres.

After the land surrenders, the Lake Simcoe and Couchiching Ojibwa (Chippewa) separated and settled in three groups — Chief John Aisance and his band around Lake Huron (they eventually settled at Beausoleil Island in Georgian Bay), Chief William Yellowhead at the Narrows, and Chief Joseph Snake on Snake Island and in Cook's Bay. The government then decided that the native population of the lakes should take up agriculture, should become Christians, and should be located together, apart from European settlers. This was to "advance the moral condition" of the indigenous people. Once more they were relocated, this time at the Narrows and on the Coldwater reserve, an agricultural settlement, so they could become more inculcated into agriculture. Government policy changed again. The reserve would be sold and the people moved to Manitoulin Island, where they would live in isolation. Snake, Yellowhead and Aisance surrendered the reserve but their people refused to go to Manitoulin. Yellowhead went to Rama, Aisance to Beausoleil (later Christian) Island, and the Snake people to the Snake Islands, which included Snake, Fox, Georgina and Thorah Islands. Gradually Chief Snake moved his people to Georgina, the largest of the islands.

The old church and school, Georgina Island.

Government policy, which involved so many relocations, had succeeded in leaving the Chippewa a disheartened people. Snake Island, their former home, had been deserted for so long that it had reverted to an unkempt state. Everything the people had done seemed to be lost. H. A. McCue concludes that the Lake Simcoe natives "were plagued with problems. Missionaries were competing for souls. The government wanted their land and their friendship. They were set upon by corrupt traders who were only too eager to exchange liquor for the annual present the people received from the government."

Teresa Big Canoe.

Of the Chippewa families who moved from Snake to the better agricultural land on Georgina — Snake, Charles, Blackbird, Bigsail, and Big Canoe — the influence of the Big Canoe family has been dominant. After the death of Joseph Snake in 1861, Simpson Bigsail became chief, then George Charles, George McCue and, in 1875, Thomas Big Canoe (his wife was Joseph Snake's daughter, Mary Louise). In the one hundred and thirty-seven years from Joseph Snake's death to this date, Big Canoe men — Thomas, Charles, John, Lorenzo, Andrew and Hugh — have served as chief for seventy-nine of those years.

Thomas Big Canoe's great-great-granddaughter, Wanda Big Canoe, lives on Georgina Island. A talented, dynamic woman, she is head of the Starwalker Foundation, which raises funds to pay for the education of gifted aboriginal young people. Her house stands beside the old home in which she was raised and in which five generations of Big Canoes have lived. In Thomas Big Canoe's time, each family had its own hunting preserve. His was Algonquin Park. Wanda remembers tales of her great-grandfather, Charles, a "benevolent dictator, who did the best for his people whether they liked it or not." A Wesleyan Methodist, he insisted upon proper Sunday dress, and was a strong believer in the work ethic. The

Chief Lorenzo Big Canoe.

Young Wanda Big Canoe.

works of Shakespeare and Bacon were in the home to be read and discussed. Wanda's father, Lorenzo Big Canoe, chief from 1959 to 1963, was "an elegant man, a good friend of John Deifenbaker. He dealt with the Department of Indian Affairs, and was much in demand as an after-dinner speaker."

Today the islands have changed. The lands on Snake Island, still owned by the native people, are leased to cottagers who have built summer homes there. They are managed by the reserve, with one member always living on the island as caretaker. The same situation exists on Fox Island. (Most of the lands on Thorah, once a Chippewa camping and hunting ground, have been sold through the Department of Indian Affairs.) The income goes for administrative purposes at the reserve on Georgina Island. The roads they built have been widened, and by their side stands the Community Hall, the Health Centre, the water treatment plant, an elementary school and church. Her people, says Wanda, have created a good home.

Wanda Big Canoe, great-great-granddaughter
of Thomas Big Canoe of the Big Canoe Chippewa chiefs.

Tranquil or turbulent, the lake has an ever-changing face.

The dock, Georgina Island, in mist.

The height of ice-fishing season.

The bounty of Holland Marsh.

Winter's artistry, Roches Point.

The Forster home, Ingleside, at Orchard Beach, built in 1896 and one of the last remaining examples of an early Lake Simcoe cottage. It boasts a resident ghost, a kindly gentleman but one who was particularly interested in the house guests and had to be admonished by the present owner for over-zealous rattling of doors. Ingleside is located in an area where the Yates family once operated a sawmill. When its usefulness was ending, Yates adapted to the times and, with wood from his mill, built nine cottages and rented them out. Novelist Mazo de La Roche, whose Jalna series was internationally popular, spent a summer here and worked in one of the cottages.

Twin cottages at Jackson's Point.

Summer hats grace the wall at Beechcroft, Roches Point.

The peacock house at The Briars, Jackson's Point.

The Briars. Its unusual tower provides a spendid view of the lake.

Susan Sibbald's great-great-great-great-grand-children in front of the Red Barn, the old Briars barn and now the longest running professional summer theatre in Canada. (The previous resident, a holstein bull was penned in what is now the men's washroom.) The barn was converted into a theatre in 1948 by Harry Kohl, architect. It is said that he was accompanied there by Harry Belafonte, who ventured into the rafters with the bats to sing. Brian Doherty was the first director. In the first season, 1949, Alfred Mulock and his actress wife, Steffi Lock, opened the doors, and Wayne and Shuster trod the boards there. They were followed by many distinguished names in theatre, actors and actresses, directors and producers — Robin Cameron, Martha Henry, Leon Major, Margot Charlesworth, Amelia Hall, Bill Glassco, Barbara Hamilton, Dinah Christie, Kate Reid, Frances Hyland, Tom Kneebone, Timothy Findley, Jennifer Phipps, Jack Duffy, Mia Anderson, Toby Robbins….

Nature's hockey rink.

Sunlight flashes back in lighter colour from the sandbar on the shoals; the passing clouds of summer throw moving shadows as over a ripening field...
STEPHEN LEACOCK

A peaceful spot to moor.

Steamer Fairy, *later* Carrie Ella, *1870–78.*
A screw steamer, 75 feet long, built by Thompson Smith at Barrie, to ply between Orillia and Washago on Lake Couchiching in connection with the stage line to Gravenhurst, before the railway reached Muskoka. She was later rebuilt by D. L. Sanson of Orillia and renamed Carrie Ella.
She was commanded by Captain Peter Lyons and later by his son Captain O. H. Lyons of Barrie.

The Lake Steamers

The ships that traversed Lakes Simcoe and Couchiching became legends. Each one had her personality, sometimes amiable, sometimes cranky and obstinate, sometimes downright explosive. They brought settlers to their new homes, and carried essential supplies and mail. And when the railroad invaded their territory, they became excursion vessels, promising daytime delights and moonlight madness. But they never promised reliability. Their temperamental machinery, their route through the shallow waters of the lakes, across sandbanks and through sudden violent changes of weather, made steamer reliability an oxymoron. Steamer passengers never knew what to expect or where they were likely to spend the night.

But the passenger steamers were the pride of the lakes. The first of the lake steamers was launched in 1832. She was the *Sir John Colborne*, named for Canada's governor-general and financed by Edward O'Brien and other half-pay officers from farms around the lake. A side-wheeler, she was built in Holland Landing. It was said that part of her role was to be ready in the event of attack by Americans. In that case it was fortunate that no such attack took place, for if speed were an element in defence, the *Colborne* would have been found lacking. Speed was not her strong point. It took her all day to go from Holland Landing to Orillia with stops at Jackson's Point and Beaverton and the same length of time to make the return trip the next day via Atherley, Barrie and Bell Ewart.

Her initial voyage, in 1832, was a triumph of impulse and necessity over schedule. It was reported in the London *Times*.

The trip from Holland Landing to Kempenfeldt consumed no less than a week, a day or two of which was spent at the mouth of Cook's Bay. Proceeding thence along the south shore calls were made at Jackson's Point and Beaverton but when the craft endeavored to make Orillia she could not pass the Lake Couchiching Narrows. A day was employed in replenishing her fuel hold but for want of a safe landing place the wood had to be brought off the shore in small boats. Continuing her course westward along the north shore of the lake halts were made at the cabin of every settler along the route as they were all stockholders in the enterprise, possessed of very convivial dispositions and only too eager to celebrate the advent of steam navigation upon Lake Simcoe. So what mattered that a week's cruise was necessary to chain the two termini. Time was not of the essence. Even though it had been many of the settlers kept a more powerful essence on tap in their cabins which accounts in some degree for the length of time spent on the pioneer cruise of the pioneer steamer over the most charming of inland Canadian water stretches.

Charles Thompson, owner of a stagecoach line and hostelries along the route from York to Holland Landing, bought the *Sir John Colborne* the year after she was built. The following year he added another side-wheeler, the *Simcoe*, to his transportation system. (She was quickly renamed for her principal shareholder, Peter Robinson, the Commissioner of Crown Lands.) She travelled somewhat faster than the deliberate speed of the *Colborne*. But the two boats were not profitable for Thompson and he converted the *Colborne* to a sailing schooner. Sadly, both vessels ended their days ignominiously, the bones of the *Sir John Colborne* lying at the bottom of the Holland River, near Bradford, and those of the *Peter Robinson* by the railway bridge at the Narrows.

Soon a competitive duo appeared: the *Beaver*, launched in 1845 at Point Mara, and the *Morning*, built five years later. Both ran from Bell Ewart to Orillia, but the *Morning* could do the jaunt in slightly less time. Up to the challenge, the *Beaver* offered to carry passengers free — and the *Morning* responded. The *Beaver* offered free meals. The *Morning* met the challenge. Each offered band music and other delights. Before they went out of business from the heady competition, both vessels were purchased by the Ontario, Simcoe and Lake Huron Union Railroad Company. The *Beaver* was retired and, ignominiously, was left to rot under the old GTR station at Barrie. The *Morning* met the same end but on a different side of the lake. Caught in a storm near Roches Point, she was swept onto a shoal and spent the winter frozen in the ice. When spring came she was cast ashore, where she rotted.

The side-wheeler touted as the fastest boat to cross the lakes was the *J. C. Morrison*, owned by the Northern Railway Company and named after her president. She was a beauty with saloon cabins on her

Anticipation of a trip — a steamer at the dock.

upper deck, furniture made by the prestigious Jacques and Hay furniture company, good meals, an enthusiastic crew, and a price tag of $60,000. She could make up to fifteen miles an hour — but she quickly got a reputation as "unwieldy, top-heavy and cranky," and even a "failure." On one of her early outings she stuck on a mud flat near the Narrows and her passengers had to extend their trip by spending a night on board. Two years after she was built the *J. C. Morrison* caught fire at dock in Barrie and had to be sent out into Kempenfeldt Bay. She lit up the night sky as she burned her way to Allandale. Her hull lies there on a sandbar.

Captain Isaac May's *Emily May* (named after his daughter) was the largest steamer ever to sail Lake Simcoe. She weighed 181 tons, was 144 feet in length and could carry upwards of 500 passengers. Built at Bell Ewart, she met the morning trains there and took passengers, mail and supplies around the lake, reaching a level of dependability never before contemplated. In 1874 she was purchased by the Northern Railway and renamed the *Lady of the Lakes*. For many she was the queen. For twenty-two years she met eager passengers at their dock, bunting flying, bands playing, with a promise of pleasure in store. In spite of this she was left in 1879 to rot at Bell Ewart, a place that, it was said by that time, "itself was crumbling into oblivion with the decline of the lumber trade and the destruction of its sawmills."

The Emily May.

By 1877, Lake Simcoe was encircled by rail lines. The days of the old steamers were ending. But the days of tourism on the lakes were beginning. Resorts were being built, and so the steamers continued to ply the lakes into the twentieth century. Among others were the *Carrie Ella*, the first steamer to be propelled by a screw, and the *Orillia*, renamed the *Islay*, the first steamer built in that town (her owner, Captain McInnes, bought Strawberry Island off Atherley and opened a small resort). The *Geneva* (1905) was the last steamer to be built on Lake Simcoe. The era of the powerboat had arrived.

But the era of the lake steamers did not die out with a whimper. The *Otonobee*, from Peterborough, came to the lakes in 1911 and had a brief career that was notable chiefly for its accidents. In an effort to revive cruises up the Holland River to Bradford, her owners sent her along that shallow course. She captured the complete attention of the locals as she churned up mud and got stuck on a sandbar. She had continual engine trouble and once, stranded in Kempenfeldt Bay, had to utter feeble toots for help. She sank at the dock in Barrie and had to be pumped out and refloated. En route up the Trent Canal she hit the swing-bridge at Bolsover and scored a direct blow on the bridge attendant's backside. She rammed into the dock at Big Cedar Point (it was rumoured that her captain and mate were drunk). It all ended for the *Otonobee* during the night of August 15, 1916. She caught fire at the Big Bay Point dock. The dock burned in the conflagration. The lighthouse caught fire and the acetylene tanks inside exploded. Needless to say, the inhabitants of the Point were rudely awakened. Some said they were sure it was Germans bombing Lake Simcoe.

Of course the most famous steamer of all never existed. She was a creation of Stephen Leacock's. He took all the eccentricities of a local steamer, the *Enterprise*, and put them together with the lakes' other equally quixotic vessels to form the *Mariposa Belle*, the lake steamer that became known through the outing of the Knights of Pythias in *Sunshine Sketches of a Little Town*. The sinking of the *Mariposa Belle* after an excursion on Lake Wissanotti (Couchiching) is a well-loved tale.

Excursion Day, at half-past six of a summer morning! With the boat all decked in flags and all the people in Mariposa on the wharf, and the band in peaked caps with big cornets tied to their bodies ready to play at any minute! I say! Don't tell me about the carnival of Venice and the Delhi Durbar. Don't! I wouldn't look at them. I'd shut my eyes! For light and colour give me every time an excursion out of Mariposa down the lake to the Indians Island out of sight in the morning mist. Talk of your Papal Zouaves and your Buckingham Palace Guard! I want to see the Mariposa band in uniform and the Mariposa Knights of Pythias with their aprons and their insignia and their picnic baskets and their five-cent cigars!

After a splendid day on the lake, the *Mariposa Belle* turned to head for home. It was then that word went around that she was sinking…

And Pepperleigh said it was a perfect scandal and passed the news on to his wife and she said that they had no business to allow it and that if the steamer sank that was the last excursion she'd go on….I'm not sure now I come to think of it that it isn't worse than sinking in the Atlantic. After all in the Atlantic there is wireless telegraphy, and a lot of trained sailors and stewards…you'd have been scared too if you'd been there just before the steamer sank, and seen them bringing up all the women to the top deck…Then, quite suddenly, with a quiver, down she went. You could feel the boat sink, sink — down, down, — would it never get to the bottom? The water came up flush up to the lower deck, and then, — thank heaven, — the sinking stopped and there was the Mariposa Belle safe and tight on a reed bed.

Rescue parties came out in response to flares of distress and then all the rescuers, exhausted by their efforts, had to be rescued. Finally the ship was refloated and made it into dock with none injured — the way, fortunately, that most aborted steamer excursions ended. Everyone in town was on the dock to greet the survivors.

Look at the lights and the crowd! If only the federal census taker could count us now! …and there's the Mariposa band, — actually forming in a circle on the upper deck just as she docks, and the leader with his baton, — one- two — ready now, — O CAN-A-DA.

The Ice City

There is a city on Lake Simcoe that ranks only behind Barrie and Orillia in size. Its population of 24,000 is transient but fiercely loyal. Its six thousand buildings are moved each March when the foundations on which they sit begin to crack. They reappear on site the following December or January. This is the city of ice huts that dot the lake, making Lake Simcoe the ice-fishing capital of the world.

Today's ice huts have heat, some have a comfortable chair or two, a television set, a radio, a rug on the floor beside the hole in the ice —not at all like what one settler saw in 1815. A native fisherman was crouched on the ice… "He had so completely enveloped himself in a large buffalo skin that no part of his body, head, hands, or feet were to be discovered. He sat over a square hole cut in the ice, with a short spear ready to transfix any fish which might be attracted by his bait. The hole was about a foot square, and the bait was an artificial fish of white wood, with leaden eyes and tin fins, and about eight or nine inches long. The ice where he had cut was about three feet thick." The Indian was spear-fishing, a method long used but now outlawed.

This "artificial fish of white wood" was the type of wooden decoy that had been used by fishermen for centuries to lure fish to within striking distance of their spears. Joe Fossey, a Barrie resident, is a decoy collector and expert carver with a lifelong interest in sport fishing and boatbuilding. He says, "The making of fish decoys for spear-fishing is a very important part of the long and rich tradition of ice fishing. There is documentary evidence that North American native people spear-fished through the ice since prehistoric times." Their decoys were hand-carved. The important part of their construction was the way in which their fins moved. They were meant to attract trout, pike or muskie by the way they swam, not by their good looks. The spears were homemade too; ranging from a sharpened stick to a hand forged weapon.

Farmers, supplementing their income, turned to commercial ice spear-fishing, building light cedar huts that they could move to follow the fish. Eventually, hut rentals were introduced to the public by ice-fishing operators, who might have their own identifiable decoy design. Spear-fishing was so successful that hundreds of tons of fish were speared each year. Eventually a movement by concerned conservationists resulted in spears being banned. That ban took effect in Lake Simcoe in 1940.

Wooden decoys are now much sought after by antique collectors. One prize decoy was discovered by Joe Fossey. It had been made in Lefroy by George Wheeler in 1913 and was patented in the United States in 1921. The patent office noted that "when the unsuspecting fish took the bait into its mouth from either side, the bottom release bar mechanism was triggered, which in turn spring released the four concealed hooks to impale the fish onto the bait."

The prime ice-fishing areas on the lake are the same today as they were in the early days — the east side of Lake Simcoe between Island Grove, Jackson's Point and Beaverton, and on the west side in Kempenfeldt Bay, Barrie and Orillia. Bob Sharp, of Dave's Fish Huts in Jackson's Point, operates a village in this ice-hut city, a village founded by his father thirty years ago. Its boundaries are marked off with trees. Bob stands behind the desk in his office, a ten-man hut located on ice over fifteen feet of water. When customers come in, he supplies them with minnows by hauling up his minnow case through a hole in the floor. It is serious fishermen he wants, not the kind who will drop beer caps down an ice hole and "spook the fish."

Ice fishing is a multimillion-dollar business now for the operators on Lake Simcoe. And it is a hazardous one for the uninitiated. Bob was initiated at the age of six when he walked seven or eight miles out on the ice for the first time with his father. It was then that he learned about the long pressure crack that follows the lake's shoreline. This fissure causes movement of the ice and forces cracks in the lake's frozen surface — deep gashes such as the "big crack" that once isolated Bob and his father. The ice on which they were standing moved, an upside-down V formed, and their section broke off. Water came up through the huge crack and took out everything in its path.

A prize catch.

Early in March each year the world ice-fishing championships take place on Lake Simcoe, attracting international competitors. Regular teams of four come from Germany, Holland, Lithuania and all over the United States and Canada, with 100 teams the limit. Teams compete for the $10,000 first prize. The events are non-profit, with proceeds going to support preservation projects in Lake Simcoe.

Ice sailing.

Carley Boats, Orillia.

The Boatbuilders

In the golden age of rowing and paddling, the lakes were full of colourful sails, and of regattas where professional oarsmen such as Ned Hanlan or Jake Gaudaur might appear. In the summer months, if the band was playing in the evening, hundreds of canoes, some decked out with cushions, blankets, backrests, and perhaps a Chinese lantern, congregated in Kempenfeldt Bay, listening to the local band and enjoying the spectacular sight they were creating. For a daytime outing, a woman needed a parasol and a stylish Victorian dress so her escort could admire her while paddling.

Rowing was in style. The waterfronts at Barrie and Orillia were lined with boat works. In Orillia, among others, were Rolland's, with sixty canoes to rent, the J. H. Ross Canoe Company, William Madill's canoes, Ditchburn's Boat Works, (formerly Hunter's), and Joseph Carley's boat business, where it is believed that world champion Jake Gaudaur got his start. A skilled yachtsman, John Carley, Joseph's brother, set up his boatbuilding shop in Barrie in 1867. Two years later the Canadian government commissioned him to

Boatbuilder William Mitchell.

build boats for the Red River Expedition. Thirty-two feet long, each boat could fit up to two masts and accommodate six oars. With this success as a start, John Carley built many types of small boats — "steam, sail, oar-or-paddle propelled, from one to eight passenger in type. In 1904 he was fitting up a 'neat little gasoline engine.'"

Another well-known name in boating was Grew Boats. Art Grew learned the boat-building business from the Ackroyd Bros. in Toronto, builders of the popular 14-foot cat-rigged dinghy. In 1907, however, Art developed respiratory problems that prompted a move north. He settled in Jackson's Point and, with his father's help, set up a business in a two-storey boathouse. In addition to renting boats and canoes, he built at least one boat in his first year there — a 20-foot gaff-rigged hull — the first of scores on the lakes. In 1932, Clarence Kemp, then owner of Grew Boats, partnered with Eric Osborne, purchased the Gibley Boat Works. Not long afterwards the two firms were consolidated in Penetanguishene under the name Grew Boats.

A Kempenfeldt Bay regatta, 1905.

J. H. Ross Boats, Orillia.

STEAMER "ISLAY."

J. H. ROSS,

. . BUILDER OF . .

HIGH-GRADE

Skiffs, Canoes and Yachts.

SAILS AND TENTS MADE TO ORDER.

Second-hand Boats and Canoes always in stock. Boats and Canoes for Hire by day or week. Prices quoted on Steam Launches upon application.

Lover's Creek, Tollendal, location of Mitchell Boat Works, circa 1895–1920.

Alvin Wice launching a Mitchell boat at Minett's Point, near Barrie, circa 1910.

And there were small boat-building enterprises. William Mitchell lived on the site of his boat works at Tollendal on Lovers' Creek. He concentrated on building quality cedar lapstrake rowing skiffs that were light and speedy, just what was needed to win the regatta rowing race. Harold Rolland, from Rolland's Boats in Orillia, recalled the day he came over to pick up twelve of Mitchell's rowing skiffs for their rental business. They tied them together "like a string of sausage" and towed them back to Orillia. And when it came to launching his skiffs, Mitchell had the answer. A team of horses were trained to walk into the water until the boat had depth enough to float.

And so, until the powerboat dominated the waters, most vessels that traversed Lakes Simcoe and Couchiching were built on their shores. Their builders were adept at creating fine crafts, from the sleek and silent canoe to the gaudy lake steamer. Initially a life-line, the lake vessels became a means for exploration, commerce, sport and leisure and, above all, they made interaction between the lakes' disparate communities possible — the communities that became a whole, with a story to tell.

Fernlea at Shanty Bay, one of the earliest summer homes on Kempenfelt Bay, was built circa 1880.
It was purchased by Frank Rolph in 1912 and sold to R. S. Waldie in 1922. It is still in the Waldie family today.

Select Bibliography

Arbuckle, Franklin, Jack Carr and Fergus Cronin. *The Group of Seven, Why Not Eight or Nine or Ten?* The Arts and Letters Club of Toronto 1995

Beaverton Thorah Eldon Historical Society. *The Beaverton Story.* Beaverton 1984

Byers, Mary, Jan Kennedy and Margaret McBurney. *Rural Roots.* University of Toronto Press 1976

Curry, Ralph L. *Stephen Leacock: Humorist and Humanist.* Doubleday, New York 1959

de Pencier, Honor. *Posted to Canada: The Watercolours of George Russell Dartnell 1835–1844.* Dundurn, Toronto 1987

Doyle, James. *Stephen Leacock, The Sage of Orillia.* ECW Press, Toronto 1992

Fisher, W. Allen. *The Genesis of Barrie 1783.1858.* Printing Unlimited, Barrie 1987

Francis, Daniel. *"I Remember…" An Oral History of the Trent-Severn Waterway.* Friends of the Trent-Severn Waterway. Peterborough 1984

French, Gary, Su Murdoch, and Irene Perri. *Barrie: A Nineteenth-Century County Town.* East Georgian Bay Historical Foundation, 1984

Gould, Glenn and John McGreevy *Glenn Gould by Himself and His Friends.* Doubleday Canada. Toronto 1983

Heidenreich, Conrad E. *"…and go to Innisfree" 100 Years at De Grassi Point.* Innisfree Limited 1989

Hett, Frances Paget. *Georgina.* The Paget Press, Sutton 1978

Hett, Frances Paget. *The Memoirs of Susan Sibbald.* The Paget Press, Sutton 1980

Hunter, A. F. *Lake Simcoe and Its Environs.* Barrie 1893

Hunter, Martha. *A History of Simcoe County.* Reprod. edition 1948. Sponsored and distributed by the Historical Committee of Simcoe County, Barrie

Leacock, Stephen. *Sunshine Sketches of a Little Town.* McClelland and Stewart, Toronto 1931

Legate, David M. *Stephen Leacock: A Biography.* Doubleday 1970

Leitch, Adelaide. *The Visible Past. The Pictorial History of Simcoe County.* County of Simcoe, 1967

MacCrimmon, Hugh R. and Elmars Skobe. *The Fisheries of Lake Simcoe.* Department of Lands and Forests, 1970

McEwen, Joanna, ed. *The Story of Oro.* Township of Oro 1987

Martyn, Carlos. *William E. Dodge The Christian Merchant.* New York 1890

Miller, Audrey Saunders, ed. *The Journals of Mary O'Brien 1828–1835.* Macmillan Co. of Canada, 1968

Moritz, Albert and Theresa. *Leacock: A Biography.* Stoddart, Toronto 1985

North-Side Nostalgia: 100 Years at De Grassi Point. 1990

Richmond, Randy. *The Orillia Spirit.* Dundurn, 1996

Vernon, J. A. H. and S. E. H. Vernon, eds. *Ladywood.* Bowne, 1992

Articles, Journals, Pamphlets and Scholarly Papers

Andrews, Robert J. Transcription of the "Field Book of William Kingdom Rains"

Buggey, Susan and John J. Stewart. "Lakehurst and Beechcroft, Roches Point, Ontario, Canada," *Journal of Garden History* Volume 1 Number 2

Cox, Elizabeth Campbell. "The Marsh Letters 1819–1836"

Department of Lands and Forests, Ontario. "Eildon Hall: Sibbald Memorial Museum" 1965

Fossey, Joe. "Ice Spearfishing Decoys," *Antique and Collectibles Trader* Volume 23 August/September 1998

____. "A Lost Lake Simcoe 'Treasure.' Fish Decoy Found Alive!" Barrie 1997

____. "Commercial Manufacturing of Canadian Fish Decoys." Barrie 1997

Fowler, Marian E. "Portrait of Susan Sibbald, Writer and Pioneer," Ontario Historical Society, *Ontario History* Volume LXVI Number 1, March 1974

Frayne, Trent. "The Erudite Jester of McGill," *Maclean's* January 1, 1953

History Committee, St. Thomas' Anglican Church, Shanty Bay. "Anniversary History"

Ironside, Allan. "The Tudhopes of Orillia," *East Georgian Bay Historical Journal* Volume 2

Leacock, Stephen. "This Lake Simcoe Country," *Canadian Geographical Journal* Volume XI Number 3, September 1935

McCue, H. A. "The Lake Simcoe Indians: A History from 1792–1876"

McKay, Donald. "The Days of the Pioneers at Big Bay Point," *Pioneer Papers* Number 3. Simcoe County Pioneer and Historical Society. Simcoe County 1910

McKenzie, Mr. and Mrs. S. S. "The Holland Marsh Story," *Trade and Transportation*

Moriarty, Catherine B. "To the Seventh Generation: The Lee Story"

Soules, Samuel Lount. "Recollection of Moses Hayter, The First Jailer of Simcoe County," *Pioneer Papers* Number 3 Simcoe County Pioneer and Historical Society. Simcoe County 1910

Township of Oro Committee. "Hills of Oro and Other Pioneer Landmarks." Township of Oro 1993

Photo Credits

TITLE PAGE
The Briars. Private collection

INTRODUCTION
6. *Penetanguishene Road near Kempenfeldt, 1838.* George Russell Dartnell. Private collection. From *Posted to Canada, The Watercolours of George Russell Dartnell* by Honor de Pencier.
8. *Residence of James Wickens, Lake Simcoe, 1836.* George Russell Dartnell. From *Posted to Canada, The Watercolours of George Russell Dartnell* by Honor de Pencier.
10. *View of Barrie*, Public Archives of Canada. C-13305
11. The old Penetanguishene Road today. Honor de Pencier.

ORILLIA
12. Orillia from the Narrows. Orillia Library Archives. O78
14. The Tudhope Carriage Company. Orillia Library Archives.
14. Tudhope motor buggy. Orillia Library Archives. O83
15. The Tudhope Carriage Company after the 1909 fire. Courtesy of the Simcoe County Archives. E 13 B1 R4B S9 SH3
16. Jacob (Jake) Gill Gaudaur. Courtesy of the Simcoe County Archives. B-1, 970-63
16. Franklin Carmichael. Orillia Library Archives. OR 118
17. Orillia's Grand Opera House. Orillia Library Archives.

STEPHEN LEACOCK
18. Stephen Leacock. Stephen Leacock Museum
20. Agnes Emma Butler Leacock. Georgina Village Museum and Archives
21. Gathering at Old Brewery Bay. Stephen Leacock Museum.
22. Leacock's boathouse. Stephen Leacock Museum.

KEMPENFELDT BAY
24–27. From *Ladywood*, eds. J. A. H. Vernon and S. E. H. Vernon.
28. Property of the Kempenfeldt Conference Centre, courtesy of Gregory L. Humble, general manager.
29. African Episcopal Church, Oro. Courtesy of the Simcoe County Archives. E8 B1R 3B S1 SL2
32. Lucius O'Brien. Courtesy of the Simcoe County Archives. B6R 3B S3 Sl1
32. *Etienne Jean, July 1, 1892* by Lucius O'Brien. Courtesy of the Simcoe County Archives. Neg. #283
32. York Simcoe Regiment on the march to Humboldt. Courtesy of the Simcoe County Archives. E6 B3 R3A-8-5

BARRIE
50. Barrie, 1875. Courtesy of the Simcoe County Archives Print Collection.
51. Grand Trunk Railway Depot, Allandale. Courtesy of the Simcoe County Archives. 991-29 E10 B1 3R 1-3
51. Lount's Castle. Courtesy of the Simcoe County Archives. E7 B4 R6B S3 SL3
52. Ardraven. Courtesy of the Simcoe County Archives. R3B S3 SL2
53. Inchiquin. Courtesy of the Simcoe County Archives. E1 B3 R6B S7 SL 1

BIG BAY POINT
54. The *Islay*. Courtesy of the Simcoe County Archives. B3 R4A S1 SH3
56–58. Private collections. Big Bay Point.

BELL EWART: ICE HARVESTING
60. Ice house at Bell Ewart under construction. Courtesy of the Simcoe County Archives. F10 G2
62. Alvin and Lorne Wice loading ice. Private collection.
62. Ice house. Bell Ewart Museum. Courtesy of the Simcoe County Archives. E1 B6 R1A S7 SH1

DE GRASSI POINT
63. Ethelwyn Walker Hunter. Private collection
64. De Grassi south-siders. Private collection.
65. George McMurrich and family. Private collection.
66. Sunday best at De Grassi. Private collection.
66. McKeggies. Private collection.

ROCHES POINT
68. Map of Roches Point as the capital of Upper Canada. York County Atlas. Public Archives of Ontario.
70. Christ Church Roches Point. Photo by Hugh Robertson, Panda Associates.
71. Lake steamer, Roches Point. Courtesy of the Simcoe County Archives. E6 B6 R3B-6-3
72. Eastbourne Golf Club. Private collection.
73. Ladies Field Day, Eastbourne Golf Club. Private collection.
73. Photographs by Turofsky, Toronto.

JACKSON'S POINT, SUTTON AND THE HISTORIC LAKESHORE
74. Ladies in their finery for an IODE meeting. Private collection.
74. The Holland Landing band at Jackson's Point. Private collection.
74. Jackson's Point. Private collection.
74. Ice house and mill, Jackson's Point. Georgina Village Museum and Archives.
76. Members of the Patterson and Bourchier families. Georgina Village Museum and Archives.
78. A gathering at The Briars. Private collection.
79. Ice farm. Photo by Hugh Robertson, Panda Associates.
80. Radial car. Georgina Village Museum and Archives.
80. Jackson's Point. Georgina Village Museum and Archives.
81. The *Enterprise*. Georgina Village Museum and Archives.
81. Radial Railway map. Private collection.

BEAVERTON
82 and 83. Courtesy of the Beaverton, Thorah, Eldon Historical Society.

TRENT CANAL
85. Modern-day Trent Canal. Photo by John de Visser

THE CHIPPEWA AND THE ISLANDS
86–89. From the archival collection in the Community Centre, Georgina Island, courtesy of Susan Hoeg.

COLOUR SECTION
100. Descendants of Susan Sibbald in front of the Red Barn. Photo by Peter Sibbald.

LAKE STEAMERS
104. The *Fairy*. Private collection.
106. Steamer at dock. Courtesy of the Simcoe County Archives. Acc. # 980-31
107. *Emily May*. Private collection.

THE ICE CITY
109 and 110. Courtesy of John Slykhuis, the *Georgina Advocate*.
111. Ice sailing. Courtesy of the Simcoe County Archives. 983-16

THE BOATBUILDERS
112. Carley Boats. Courtesy of the Simcoe County Archives. B2 R3B S1 SH2
113. Boatbuilder William Mitchell. Private collection.
114. A Kempenfeldt Bay regatta. Courtesy of the Simcoe County Archives. E9 B11A-9-5 986-62
114. J. H. Ross Boats. Orillia Library Archives. OR 428
114. Lover's Creek, Tollendal. Private collection.
115. Alvin Wice launching a Mitchell boat. Private collection.

116. Fernlea, Shanty Bay. Private collection.

Acknowledgments

Lake Simcoe's waters touch on communities large and small whose history is linked more to the townships that stretch back from the shore than to each other. But diverse as they are, their past has influenced their present. In each area I found people dedicated to delving into days gone by and willing to share some of their findings with me.

Kempenfeldt Bay has a history of its own, shaped by its geography. In Barrie, Su Murdoch, whose knowledge of her area is thorough and perceptive, is one of the authors of *Barrie: A Nineteenth-Century County Town*. She is also the owner of one of the oldest houses in Barrie, the home of Frederic Gore, headmaster of the Grammar School. She shared her enthusiasm with me and guided my research in Barrie. Barrie is also the home of Joe Fossey, an expert in the history of boatbuilding, ice fishing, and decoys. Acknowledged as an authority on these subjects, his informative articles have appeared in numerous North American publications. He introduced me to the art and history of spear-fishing and decoys and the special skill needed in carving these delicate lures. Joe also assisted me in obtaining early photographs, in particular those kindly loaned by Mrs. Lorne Wice.

The wit and wiles of Stephen Leacock come alive again in his home and boathouse on Lake Couchiching. Reentering the world of Mariposa/Orillia brings back memories of the sinking of the *Mariposa Belle* and the host of Orillia's notables who, like it or not, made it into the pages of *Sunshine Sketches of a Little Town*. In the Stephen Leacock Museum, Daphne Mainprize, curator, and Christina Martin, executive assistant, helped me obtain some of Leacock's writing on Simcoe and Couchiching, lakes that for him outshone the Aegean and, in fact, any other location you could name. Nena Mardsen, historian in Sutton, gave me the benefit of her scholarly research on Leacock done close to Leacock's first home, in Egypt, near Sutton. In the Orillia Public Library, Jennifer Murrant guided me through their extensive and significant collection of archival photographs. Gail Crawford, the author of *A Fine Line* (Dundurn 1998), has a special interest in and has researched the history of the Tudhope Carriage Company, one of Orillia's remarkable entrepreneurial adventures. She gave me the benefit of her work. My thanks go to Judith Adams Huot for allowing me to read the letters written to and by her great-great-grandparents, Susannah Brown Marsh and William Marsh, part of which were written at the Narrows between Lake Simcoe and Lake Couchiching.

John Vernon, a descendant of George W. Allan of Strathallan and Herbert and Maye Harcourt Vernon of Ladywood, with his wife, Sue, generously gave of their time and knowledge of the south shore of Kempenfeldt Bay. They allowed me to use photographs from their book *Ladywood*, published by Patrick Vernon, gave me a tour of that grand old Lake Simcoe home, since demolished, and introduced me to the Hogarth house, now the Kempenfeldt Conference Centre. There I met Gregory L. Humble, the general manager, who assisted me with information and photographs. In Shanty Bay, Gracie Wright, whose family has summered there for ninety years, welcomed me into her home and showed me Kempenfeldt's north shore, its grand houses, the location of the historic O'Brien dwelling, and talked of the history of the Black community there, while Joy Waldie added her own recollections.

Here and in other parts of Simcoe County, the Simcoe County Archives was an invaluable resource. Ellen Millar, assistant archivist, helped me locate the material I needed, as did Christopher Sax, archival technician.

In 1999, Big Bay Point is celebrating the seventy-fifth anniversary of its golf club, the focal point of that vital old summer place, always one of the most desirable points on Lake Simcoe. Austin Winch, longtime knowledgeable resident and local historian, talked to me about the earliest days on the Point and directed me to resources. Don Avery, custodian of the extensive work done for their commemorative book, shared the results of interviews done with cottagers and residents at the Point. I am grateful to him for his guidance and to Elizabeth "Liz" Gooch Bertram, granddaughter of F. H. Gooch, for letting me read her grandfather's journals.

On De Grassi Point, both "north siders," and "south-siders" have strong ties to their summer homes. Jim Roberts, a north-sider, took me on a walking tour of the area, the first site visited by John Graves Simcoe in 1793, now unique as a small family-run community, and gave me photographs of his feisty ancestor, George McMurrich. Residents on the south side are all descended from Sir Byron Edmund Walker, who founded the Royal Ontario Museum, the Art Gallery of Ontario, the National Gallery in Ottawa, and the Champlain Society — no mean legacy. This was the subject of a conversation with Conrad E. Heidenreich, professor of geography at York University, and author of "…and go to Innisfree," 100 Years at De Grassi Point. Longtime friends Phil and Wendy Gilbert, and Kitty Stevens, cleared the way with introductions.

I have known Nena Marsden, scholarly local historian, since I became a volunteer in the Inventory of Historic Buildings organized by Professor William Goulding of the Faculty of Architecture, University of Toronto, some thirty years ago. I cherish these years of a shared interest and thank her for her help and encouragement with this book. At the Georgina Archives, Marg Godfrey helped me locate photographs and research material. She gave me countless hours of her time and much good advice. I contacted John Slykhuis of the Georgina Advocate for help with photographs of champion ice-fishermen and he provided me with great shots. At Orchard Beach, Rod and Barbara Maxwell, whose cottage, Ingleside, is one of the oldest on the lake, welcomed John de Visser and me. They are happy to own a heritage building that boasts a contented ghost willing to accommodate himself to Barbara's instructions that he must not disturb her guests. Also at Orchard Beach, Adele Deacon, whose roots there go back to summers in the original Yates cottages, told me of those summers. Hugh and Bernice Smythe shared photographs and stories of the Orchard Beach Golf Club.

Sutton, Jackson's Point, and the old Lakeshore Road that winds along from Jackson's Point by the Hedge Road and The Briars, are communities that were the chosen homes of retired military officers who created a bit of England and Scotland in manor houses in the colonies Pat Anderson Stanojevic, a descendant of the Bourchier family of ancient and distinguished lineage, provided me with insights into the lives of the first residents of that area. David Ross, of Lee Farm, introduced me to diaries that brought to life the travails of Captain Simon Lee and Martha Ready Smith Lee as they settled into what was still wilderness farming. Along the east shore of Lake Simcoe, in Beaverton, Jim White, Aimie Davidson and Helen Alsop met with me in the restored buildings of which they are so proud and talked of the old days in that prominent port community.

It was a fascinating experience to meet Wanda Big Canoe, a talented woman who makes things happen. I visited her twice on the Georgina Island Reserve. She talked to me about the history of her people and introduced me to her brother, Andrew Big Canoe, a former chief, who gave me information about the Big Canoe family tree. Susan Hoeg provided me with photographs and Cynthia Wesley read drafts of my work.

John Sibbald, host of The Briars, and Barbara, whose judgement and charm make the resort run smoothly, are old friends of mine. I have talked about this book for years with John, a descendant of Susan Sibbald, and have had the benefit of his counsel on many occasions. He loves Lake Simcoe, is immersed in its history, and kindly loaned me photographs from his personal archival collection.

It is an absolute delight working with the talented, artistic, energetic, adventurous, keen-witted John de Visser. We toured the lake for a photo-graphing session with Joy and Paul Nichols. Then, when John decided to get a plane for some aerial shots, I was tempted to join him until I discovered he intended to take off the window and lean out. His sense of adventure is greater than mine.

Mary Byers